Contents

8

46

10

48

54

9

30

8

The Basic K1, P1 Rib Mitten.............2
Earn Your Stripes......................5
Fill-in Basic Mitten Pattern............6
Mix It Up...............................8
Chevron Mittens........................12
Fair Isle Mittens......................14
Honeycomb Mittens......................16
Thick & Thin Striped Mittens...........18
Cabled Mittens.........................20
Striped Mittens........................22
Long Cabled Mittens....................24
Heart Motif Mittens....................26
Wave-Patterned Mittens.................28
Slip Stitch Mitts......................30
Shell Rib Wristlets....................32
Ribbed Fingerless Mitts................34
Meow Meow Mitts........................36
Ring Around the Wristers...............38
Leaf Rib Wristers......................40
Cuffed Wristers........................42
Out of Line Mitts......................44
Hourglass Mitts........................46
Tiny Bows Wristlets....................48
Ribbed Mitts...........................50
Fur-Trimmed Mitts......................52
Eyelet Rib Wristers....................54
Techniques.............................55
Embroidery.............................56

The Basic K1, P1 Rib Mitten

While there are many ways to knit mittens, let's start with the most common version: from the cuff to fingertips, worked in the round over double-pointed needles. The basic process is as follows:

1
Knitting mittens in rounds on 4 dpn (plus 1 working needle) eliminates the need for most seaming. Work the ribbing first, followed by increases up to the base of the thumb. Place the thumb sts on a piece of scrap yarn.

2
After knitting the hand, stitches are decreased to shape the top of the mitten. Work an SKP decrease to lean to the left and a k2tog decrease to lean to the right. When all decreases are made, cut the yarn and thread it through the remaining stitches, pull tightly to gather and fasten off.

3
To knit the thumb, divide the stitches over 3 dpn and pick up and knit a few stitches on the hand of the mitten to avoid creating a hole. To get a good fit, knit in rounds until the piece covers half the thumbnail. Then, work the final decreases and close as for the top of the mitten.

OPEN TOP MITTENS

Fingerless Mittens are worked in the same way as mittens, except you bind off once you get to the decreases for the hand and thumb. Doing this creates the openings for your fingers and thumb.

Wristers, also called **Wristlets**, are usually worked in rows, instead of in rounds, and have no thumb gusset. Once the knitting is complete, you end up with a straight piece of fabric that is then seamed along one edge, leaving an opening for the thumb.

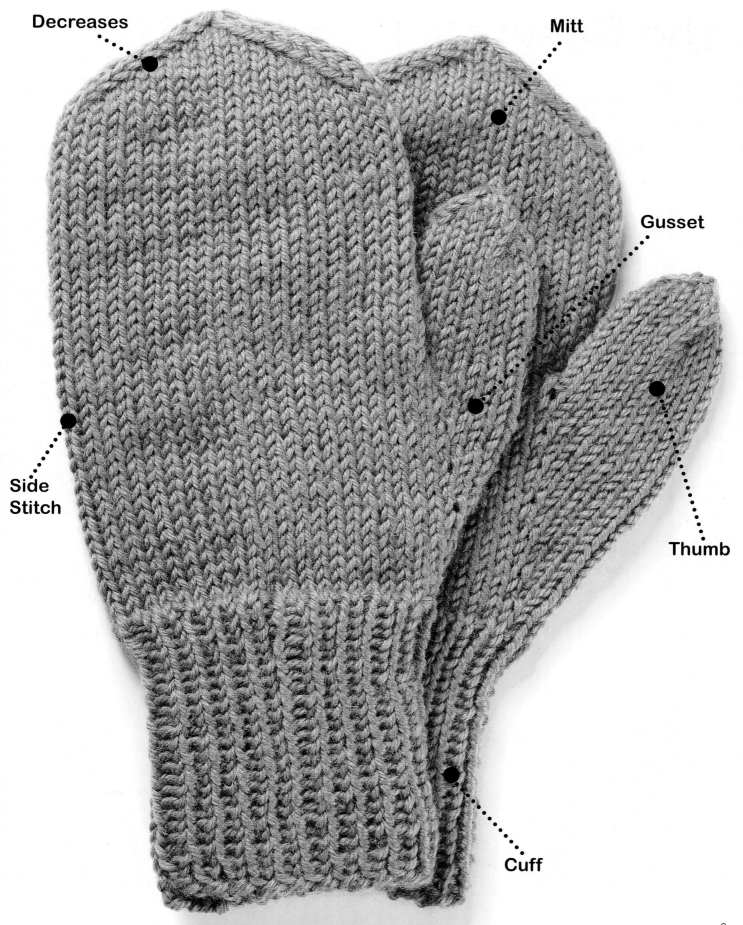

Basic K1, P1 Mitten Pattern

Easy

SIZES
Child (Woman, Man).

MEASUREMENTS
Length (wrist to fingertips) 7 (10, 11)"/18 (25.5, 28)cm
Wrist circumference 5¼ (6½, 7½)"/13.5 (16.5, 19)cm

MATERIALS
Yarn (4)
- 6oz/170g, 312yd/285m of any worsted weight acrylic yarn in Blue

Needles
- One set (5) size 6 (4mm) double-pointed needles (dpn), *or size to obtain gauge*

Notions
- Stitch markers
- Scrap yarn

GAUGE
20 sts and 28 rows to 4"/10cm over St st using size 6 (4mm) needles.
TAKE TIME TO CHECK YOUR GAUGE.

LEFT MITTEN
Cast on 32 (40, 48) sts and divide evenly over 4 dpn. Join, take care not to twist sts, and pm for beg of rnd.
Rnd 1 *K1, p1; rep from * to end.
Rep rnd 1 for k1, p1 rib for 2 (3, 3)"/5 (7.5, 7.5)cm.
Cont in St st (k every rnd) for 3 rnds.

Begin Thumb Gusset
Rnd 1 K12 (16, 20), pm, M1R, k2, M1L, pm, k to end—2 sts inc'd.
Rnds 2 and 3 Knit.
Rnd 4 K to marker, sm, M1R, k to marker, M1L, sm, k to end—36 (44, 52) sts.
Rnds 5–13 Rep rnds 2–4 three times more—42 (50, 58) sts.

For Woman and Man Sizes Only
Rnds 14 and 15 Knit.
Rnd 16 K to marker, sm, M1R, k to marker, M1L, k to end—(52, 60) sts.

Rnd 17 Knit.

For Man Size Only
Rnds 18 and 19 Knit.
Rnd 20 K to marker, sm, M1R, k to marker, sm, M1L, k to end—62 sts.
Rnd 21 Knit.

For All Sizes
Next rnd K12 (16, 20), remove marker, place next 12 (14, 16) sts on scrap yarn for thumb, cast on 2 sts, remove marker, k to end—32 (40, 48) sts.
Cont in St st on 32 (40, 48) sts for hand of mitten until piece is 5½ (8½, 9½)"/14 (21.5, 24)cm, or until hand is long enough to cover index fingernail.

Shape Top
Rnd 1 [K1, SKP, k10 (14, 18), k2tog, k1] twice—28 (36, 44) sts.
Rnd 2 [K1, SKP, k8 (12, 16), k2tog, k1] twice—24 (32, 40) sts.
Cont in this manner, dec'ing 4 sts each rnd and knitting 2 sts fewer between each set of decreases until there are 2 sts between dec's—12 sts for all sizes.
Final rnd [K1, SKP, k2tog, k1] twice—8 sts for all sizes.
Cut yarn, leaving long tail. Pull tail through rem sts, draw up, and secure.

Thumb
Pick up 5 (6, 7) sts from 12 (14, 16) sts on scrap yarn with first dpn, 5 (6, 7) sts with 2nd dpn, and 2 sts with 3rd dpn; pick up and k 2 sts from hand of mitten with 3rd dpn—14 (16, 18) sts. Join and pm for beg of rnd.
Work even in St st until thumb measures 1¼ (2, 2¼)'/3.5 (5, 6)cm, or long enough to cover half of thumbnail.
Next row [K2tog, k1] 4 (5, 6) times, k2 (1, 0)—10 (11, 12) sts.
Next row [K2tog] 5 (5, 6) times, k0 (1, 0)—5 (6, 6) sts.
Next row [K2tog] 2 (3, 3) times, k1 (0, 0)—3 sts.
Cut yarn, leaving long tail. Pull tail through rem sts, draw up, and secure.

FINISHING
Weave in ends. Block to measurements.

RIGHT MITTEN
Work as for left mitten until begin thumb gusset.
Rnd 1 K18 (22, 26), pm, M1R, k2, M1L, pm, k to end—34 (42, 50) sts.
Complete as for left mitten.•

Earn Your Stripes

Now that you understand the basic construction of knitting mittens, you can move on to something even more fun—stripes! Follow the basic pattern from page 4, but mix it up by using multiple colors throughout. Here are three examples of how you can do that, but you can always add stripes or colorblock however you please as long as you follow the basic pattern.

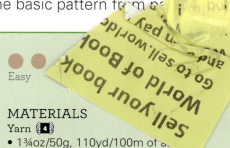

Easy

MATERIALS
Yarn [4]
- 1¾oz/50g, 110yd/100m of a worsted weight acrylic

Needles
- One set (5) size 7 (4.5mm) double-pointed needles (dpn), *or size to obtain gauge*

Notions
- Stitch markers
- Scrap yarn

SIZES
Child (Woman, Man). Shown in Woman's size.

MEASUREMENTS
Length (wrist to fingertips) 7 (10, 11)"/18 (25.5, 28)cm
Hand circumference 6½ (8, 9½)"/16.5 (20.5, 24)cm

GAUGE
20 sts and 28 rows to 4"/10cm over St st using size 7 (4.5mm) needles.
TAKE TIME TO CHECK YOUR GAUGE.

Line It Up

Yarn
1 skein each in Red (A), Navy (B), and Variegated Orange (C)

Mittens
Work as for Basic K1, P1 Rib Mitten Pattern (see page 4) with the following changes: Work ribbing with A; work hand in alternating 6-row stripes of B and C; work top portion of thumb with A.•

Jazzy Bands

Yarn
1 skein each in Orange (A) and Yellow (B)

Mittens
Work as for Basic K1, P1 Rib Mitten Pattern (see page 4) with the following changes: Work entire piece in a 2-row alternating stripe pattern of A and B.•

Block Party

Yarn
1 skein each in White (A), Green (B), Yellow (C), and Orange (D)

Mittens
Work as for Basic K1, P1 Rib Mitten Pattern (see page 4) with the following changes: Work rib with A; 28 rnds of hand and up to base of thumb with B; remainder of hand with C; top of thumb with D.•

Mittens for All!

This customizable pattern enables you to make mittens for children, women, and men using three common yarn weights: DK, worsted, and bulky.

Simply fill in the blanks in the pattern below using the chart on the next page for the appropriate yarn weight and size. Be sure to use the suggested needle size or whatever size that allows you to match the required gauge.

Note that you can work the entire pattern in a single color using only 1 or 2 skeins, or you can create any of the simple variations on pages 8 and 9 using 1 skein of each color.

Fill-In Basic K2, P2 Rib Mitten Pattern

Easy

SIZES
Child (Woman, Man).

MEASUREMENTS
Hand circumference
6 (7½, 9)"/15 (19, 23)cm
Length 7 (9½, 11½)"/17.5 (24, 29)cm

MATERIALS

DK Weight 3
- 1¾oz/50g, 130yd/117m of any DK weight wool
- One set (5) size 6 (4mm) dpn, *or size to obtain gauge*

Worsted Weight 4
- 1¾oz/50g, 110yd/100m of any worsted weight wool
- One set (5) size 8 (5mm) dpn, *or size to obtain gauge*

Bulky Weight 5
- 1¾oz/50g, 65yd/59m of any bulky weight wool
- One set (5) size 10 (6mm) dpn, *or size to obtain gauge*

All Weights
- Stitch markers
- Stitch holder or scrap yarn

GAUGES
- 22 sts and 30 rnds to 4"/10cm over St st using **DK Weight** yarn and size 6 (4mm) needles.
- 16 sts and 24 rnds to 4"/10cm over St st using **Worsted Weight** yarn and size 8 (5mm) needles.
- 14 sts and 17 rnds to 4"/10cm over St st using **Bulky Weight** yarn and size 10 (6mm) needles.

TAKE TIME TO CHECK YOUR GAUGE.

Follow the chart on page 7 for the desired yarn weight and size. Left and right mittens are worked in the same way.

NOTES
1) When changing colors in ribbing, always work first rnd of new color in St st.
2) Some sizes work shaping differently on some rows. Look for the * in the pattern and on the chart on page 7.

Cast on __ sts and divide over 4 dpn. Join, taking care not to twist sts, and pm for beg of rnd.
Rnd 1 *K2, p2; rep from * to end.
Rep rnd 1 for k2, p2 rib for __"/__cm.
Cont in St st (K every rnd) until piece measures __"/__ from rib.

Begin Thumb Gusset
Next rnd K__, pm, M1R, k__, M1L, pm, k to end.
Work 2 rnds even.
Next rnd K__, sm, M1R, k to marker, M1L, sm, k to end.
Work 2 rnds even.
Rep last 3 rnds __ times.
Next rnd K__, cast on __, sl __ sts to scrap yarn, remove marker, k to end.
Work 2 rnds even.
***Next rnd** K__, ssk, k__, k2tog, k to end.
Work 2 rnds even.

Shape Top
***Next rnd** K__, ssk, k2tog, k to end.
Work __ rnds even.
Next rnd [K2, k2tog, k__, ssk, pm, k__] twice. Work 2 rnds even.
Next dec rnd [K2, k2tog, k to 2 sts before marker, ssk, sm, k __] twice. Work 1 rnd even.
Rep last 2 rnds __ times.
Rep dec rnd __ times.
Cut yarn, leaving long tail. Pull tail through rem sts, draw up, and secure.

Thumb
Pick up 1 st each side of thumb opening and __ sts along cast-on edge.
K across __ sts from holder.
Next rnd K1, ssk, k__, k2tog, k to end.
Work 1 rnd even.
***Next rnd** K1, ssk, k2tog, k around.
K __ rnds even.
Cut yarn, leaving long tail. Pull tail through rem sts, draw up, and secure.

FINISHING
Weave in ends, closing up any gaps around thumb (as necessary).
Block to measurements.•

Fill-In Basic K2, P2 Rib Mitten Chart

Instructions / Directions	DK Child	DK Woman	DK Man	Worsted Child	Worsted Woman	Worsted Man	Bulky Child	Bulky Woman	Bulky Man
Cast on __ sts, divide over dpn, join, and pm.	32	40	48	24	32	36	20	28	32
Work k2, p2 rib for __"/__ cm.	1¾/4.5	2¼/5.5	2¾/7	1¾/4.5	2¼/5.5	2¾/7	1¾/4.5	2¼/5.5	2¾/7
Cont in St st for __"/ __ cm.	½/1.5	¾/2	¾/2	½/1.5	¾/2	¾/2	½/1.5	¾/2	¾/2
K __, pm, M1R, . . .	15	18	23	11	14	16	9	13	15
. . . k __, M1L, pm, k to end. Work 2 rnds even.	4	5	6	3	4	4	3	4	4
K __, sm, M1R, k to marker, M1L, sm, k to end. Work 2 rnds even.	15	18	23	11	14	16	9	13	15
Rep last 3 rnds __ times.	2	3	4	2	3	3	1	2	3
K __, . . .	16	19	24	12	15	17	10	14	16
. . cast on __, . . .	6	7	7	5	6	6	5	5	5
. . . sl __ sts to holder, k to end. Work 2 rnds even.	8	11	13	7	10	10	5	7	9
K __, ssk, . . .	16	19	24	12	15	17	10	14	16
. . . k __, k2tog, k to end. Work 2 rnds even.	1	2	2	1	2	2	1	1	1
K __, ssk, k2tog, k to end.	16*	19	24	12*	15	17	10*	14*	16*
Work __ rnds even.	8	13	18	8	12	16	1	4	5
[K2, k2tog, k __, ssk, pm, . . .	8	12	16	5	8	10	3	7	9
. . . k __] twice. Work 2 rnds even.	1	2	2	1	2	2	1	1	1
[K2, k2tog, k to 2 sts before marker, ssk, sm, k __] twice (dec rnd). Work 1 rnd even.	1	2	2	0	2	2	1	1	1
Rep last 2 rnds __ times.	1	2	3	1	1	2	0	1	1
Rep dec rnd __ times.	1	3	4	0	2	2	1	1	2
CUT YARN, LEAVING LONG TAIL. PULL TAIL THROUGH REM STS, DRAW UP, AND SECURE.									
Pick up 1 st each side of thumb opening and k __ sts along cast-on edge.	6	7	7	5	6	6	5	5	5
K across __ sts from holder.	8	11	13	7	10	10	5	7	9
K1, ssk, k __, k2tog, k to end. Work 1 rnd even.	1	2	2	1	2	2	1	1	1
K1, ssk, k2tog, k to end.	*			*			*	*	*
K __ rnds even.	7	9	14	6	7	10	3	5	7

* Work an SK2P instead of the ssk, k2tog

Mix It Up

This section contains 9 patterns that you can make from the Fill-In Basic K2, P2 Mitten Pattern on pages 6 and 7. While each example is for a specific yarn weight and size, you can adapt the concept of the design to any yarn weight and size by adjusting the proportions and placement of the stripes or embroidery. You can even use these designs as inspiration for your own!

DK Weight Mittens

Green Thumbs

SIZE Man

YARN DK weight yarn, 1 skein each in Off-White (A) and Green (B)

MITTEN
Work Fill-In Basic K2, P2 Mitten Pattern (see pages 6 and 7) with the following changes: Begin mitten in A and work for 15 rnds more after ribbing. Work 2 rnds in B, 2 rnds in A, 19 rnds in B, 2 rnds in A, and 2 rnds in B. Complete with A. Work thumb in B.

Let It Snow

SIZE Woman

YARN DK weight yarn, 1 skein each in Off-White (A) and Green (B)

MITTEN
Work Fill-In Basic K2, P2 Mitten Pattern (see pages 6 and 7) with the following changes: Begin mitten in A and work 2 rnds. Complete mitten and thumb in B. With A, use duplicate st (see page 56) to create chart onto backs of mittens.

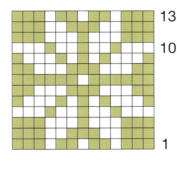

Warm Hearts

SIZE Child

YARN DK weight yarn, 1 skein each in Green (A) and Off-White (B)

MITTEN
Work Fill-In Basic K2, P2 Mitten Pattern (see pages 6 and 7) with the following changes: Begin mitten in A and work until ribbing is completed. Complete mitten and thumb in B. With 2 strands of A held tog, embroider hearts on backs of mittens in chain st (see page 56).

COLOR KEY
☐ Duplicate st in A
▨ B

Worsted Weight Mittens

Headful of Stripes

SIZE Man

YARN Worsted weight yarn, 1 skein each in Aqua (A) and Lilac (B)

MITTEN
Work Fill-In Basic K2, P2 Mitten Pattern (see pages 6 and 7) with the following changes: Begin in A and work 2 rnds. Work in B to complete ribbing and then 17 rnds more. Work [3 rnds in A, 2 rnds in B] four times, then 3 rnds in A. Complete mitten in B. Work thumb to correspond to stripes on hand.

Cozy Posies

SIZE Woman

YARN Worsted weight yarn, 1 skein each in Aqua (A) and Lilac (B)

MITTEN
Work Fill-In Basic K2, P2 Mitten Pattern (see pages 6 and 7) with the following changes: Begin in A and work ribbing, then complete mitten and thumb in B. With A, and using photo for reference, embroider flowers on backs of mittens with 5 lazy daisy petals and a large French knot center. (See page 56).

Between the Lines

SIZE Child

YARN Worsted weight yarn, 1 skein each in Lilac (A) and Aqua (B)

MITTEN
Work Fill-In Basic K2, P2 Mitten Pattern (see pages 6 and 7) with the following changes: Begin in A and work until rib is complete, then work [4 rnds in B, 1 rnd in A] to end of mitten. Work thumb to correspond to stripes on hand.

Bulky Weight Mittens

Papa Bear

SIZE Man

YARN Bulky weight yarn, 1 skein in Variegated Purple

MITTEN Work Fill-In Basic K2, P2 Mitten Pattern (see pages 6 and 7).

Mama Bear

SIZE Woman

YARN Bulky weight yarn, 1 skein in Lilac

MITTEN Work Fill-In Basic K2, P2 Mitten Pattern (see pages 6 and 7).

Baby Bear

SIZE Child

YARN Bulky weight yarn, 1 skein in Variegated Green

MITTEN Work Fill-In Basic K2, P2 Mitten Pattern (see pages 6 and 7).

Next Level Mittens

Now that you are well acquainted with basic mitten construction, it's time to expand your skills by trying some variations. The following section contains patterns that incorporate textures, cables, colorwork, different constructions, and much more.

Chevron Mittens

Easy

SIZE
Adult Woman.

MEASUREMENTS
Hand circumference 7"/19cm
Length 10½"/26.5cm

MATERIALS
Yarn
3½oz/100g, 310yd/285m of any DK weight wool in variegated blues/greens

Needles
- One set (5) each size 4 and 5 (3.5 and 3.75mm) double-pointed needles (dpn), *or size to obtain gauge*

Notions
- Stitch markers
- Scrap yarn

GAUGE
24 sts and 36 rnds to 4"/10cm over St st using larger needles.
TAKE TIME TO CHECK YOUR GAUGE.

STITCH GLOSSARY
Kyok K next st but keep st on LH needle, yo, k into same st on LH needle—2 sts inc'd.

CHEVRON PATTERN
(over 15 sts)
Rnd 1 Ssk, k5, kyok, k5, k2tog.
Rnd 2 Purl.
Rep rnds 1 and 2 for chevron pat.

MITTEN
With smaller dpn, cast on 46 sts and divide over 4 dpn (11 sts, 11 sts, 12 sts, 12 sts). Join, taking care not to twist sts, and pm for beg of rnd.
Rnd 1 *K1, p1; rep from * around.
Rep rnd 1 for k1, p1 rib until cuff measures 2"/5cm from beg.
Change to larger dpn.
Inc rnd *K3, M1, k6, M1, k5, M1, k6, M1, k3; rep from * once more—54 sts.

Begin Chevron Pattern
Rnd 1 *K6, work chevron pat over 15 sts, k6; rep from * once more.
Rep rnd 1 until mitten measures 4"/10cm from beg.

Begin Tumb Gusset
Rnd 1 Work 26 sts in pat, pm, kfb, pm, work in pat to end—55 sts.
Rnd 2 Work in pat to marker, sm, k to next marker, sm, work in pat to end.
Rnd 3 Work in pat to marker, sm, kfb, k to 1 st before next marker, kfb, sm, work in pat to end—2 sts inc'd.
Rep rnds 2 and 3 nine times more—75 sts in total, 21 between thumb markers.
Rep rnd 2 once more. Remove thumb markers.
Next rnd Work 27 sts in pat, place next 21 sts on scrap yarn, pm, work in pat to end—54 sts.
Cont working pats as established until mitten measures 9"/23cm from beg, end with a rnd 2 rep of chevron pat.

Shape Top
Rnd 1 *Ssk, work in pat to marker, k2tog, sm; rep from * once more—4 sts dec'd.
Rnd 2 Work even in pat.
Rep rnds 1 and 2 four times more—34 sts. Remove markers. Cut yarn, leaving a 20"/51cm tail, and place sts on scrap yarn, dividing front and back of mitten.

Thumb
Place 7 thumb st on each of 3 larger dpn. Pick up and k 1 st from hand edge, pm for beg of rnd—22 sts.
Rnds 1–12 Knit.
Rnd 13 [K2tog] 11 times—11 sts.
Rnd 14 Knit.
Rnd 15 K1, [k2tog] 5 times—6 sts.
Cut yarn, leaving long tail. Pull tail through rem sts, draw up, and secure.

FINISHING
Turn mitten inside out. Divide held sts evenly over two needles (for front and back of mitten). Using tail and smaller needles, join sts using the 3-Needle Bind-Off (see page 55).
Weave in ends. Block to measurements. Rep from beg for 2nd mitten.•

Design Note
These mittens are identical, meaning you can make the left and right mittens in the exact same way. There is no need to adjust for thumb placement.

Fair Isle Mittens

Intermediate

SIZE
Adult Woman.

MEASUREMENTS
Hand circumference 8"/20.5cm
Length 7"/18cm

MATERIALS
Yarn
• 1¾oz/50g, 125yd/114m of any DK weight wool in Gray Heather (A) and Red (B)

Needle
• One set (4) each size 5 and 6 (3.75 and 4mm) double-pointed needles (dpn), *or size to obtain gauge*

Notions
• Stitch markers
• Scrap yarn

GAUGE
20 sts and 32 rnds to 4"/10cm over St st using larger needles.
TAKE TIME TO CHECK YOUR GAUGE.

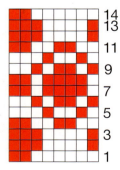

8-st rep

COLOR KEY
☐ A
■ B

RIGHT MITTEN
With smaller dpn and B, cast on 40 sts and divide evenly over 4 dpn. Join, taking care not to twist sts, and pm for beg of rnd. Cut B. Join A.
Rnd 1 *K2, p2; rep from * around.
Rep rnd 1 for k2, p2 rib for 1"/2.5cm. Join B. Knit 1 rnd. Cut B.
Join A and cont in k2, p2 rib until cuff measures 2"/5cm from beg.
Change to larger dpn and work in St st (k every rnd) for 1"/2.5cm.

Begin Thumb Gusset
Rnd 1 Knit.
Rnd 2 K2, pm, M1R, pm, k to end—41 sts.
Rnd 3 Knit.
Rnd 4 K2, sm, M1R, k to marker, M1L, sm, k to end—2 sts inc'd.
Rnds 5 and 6 Knit.
Rep rnds 4–6 five times more—53 sts in total, 13 between thumb markers. Remove thumb markers.
Next rnd K2, place 13 sts for thumb on scrap yarn, k18, pm, k to end—40 sts.

Begin Chart
Cont in St st (k every rnd) as foll:
Next rnd Work rnd 1 of chart, working 8-st rep 5 times around. Cont in this way until all 14 rnds of chart have been worked. Cut B.
With A, knit 2 rnds—piece measures approx 7½"/19cm from beg.

Shape Top
Dec rnd 1 [K2, ssk, k to 4 sts before marker, k2tog, k2] twice—4 sts dec'd.
Rnds 2 and 3 Knit.
Rep rnds 1–3 once, then rep rnds 1 and 2 three times—20 sts.
Rep rnd 1 twice more—12 sts.
Place 6 front sts on one needle and 6 back sts on a 2nd needle.
Cut yarn, leaving long tail, and graft rem sts closed using Kitchener st (see page 55).

Thumb
With larger dpn, pick up and k 2 sts along hand edge, pm, k 13 thumb sts, pick up and k 3 sts from hand edge, k to marker—18 sts.
Divide sts evenly over 3 dpn.
Rnd 1 K1, ssk, k to last 3 sts, k2tog, k1—16 sts.
Work in St st until thumb measures 1½"/4cm.
Next rnd [K2tog] 8 times—8 sts.
Next rnd Knit.
Next rnd [K2tog] 4 times—4 sts.
Cut yarn, leaving long tail. Pull tail through rem sts, draw up, and secure.

FINISHING
Weave in ends. Block lightly to measurements.

LEFT MITTEN
Work as for right mitten to thumb gusset.

Begin Thumb Gusset
Rnd 1 Knit.
Rnd 2 K18, pm, M1R, pm, k to end—41 sts.
Rnd 3 Knit.
Rnd 4 K18, sm, M1R, k to marker, M1L, sm, k to end—2 sts inc'd.
Rnds 5–6 Knit.
Rep rnds 4–6 five times more—53 sts in total, 13 between markers.
Next rnd K18, place 13 sts for thumb on scrap yarn, k2, pm, k to end—40 sts.
Complete as for right mitten. •

Design Note
The flat tops of these mittens are created using the Kitchener Stitch, a method of grafting together live sets of stitches for a seamless finish.

Honeycomb Mittens

Intermediate

SIZE
Adult Woman.

MEASUREMENTS
Hand circumference 8"/20.5cm
Length 10"/25.5cm

MATERIALS
Yarn
• 3½oz/100g, 416yd/380m of any fingering weight superwash wool/nylon blend in Pink

Needles
• One set (5) each size 1 and 2 (2.25 and 2.75mm) double-pointed needles (dpn), *or size to obtain gauge*

Notions
• Cable needle (cn)
• Stitch markers
• Scrap yarn

GAUGE
30 sts and 40 rnds to 4"/10cm over St st using larger needles.
TAKE TIME TO CHECK YOUR GAUGE.

STITCH GLOSSARY
4-st RC Sl 2 sts to cn and hold to back, k2, k2 from cn.
4-st LC Sl 2 sts to cn and hold to front, k2, k2 from cn.

RIGHT MITTEN
With smaller needles, cast on 60 sts and divide sts evenly over 4 dpn. Join, taking care not to twist sts, and pm for beg of rnd.
Rnd 1 *K2, p2; rep from * around.
Rep rnd 1 for k2, p2 rib for 2¾"/7cm. At end of last rnd, remove beg of rnd marker, knit first st of next rnd, replace beg of rnd marker. Marker is now between 2 knit sts.
Next rnd Work 30 sts in rib, pm, k4, pfb, k4, pfb, k8, pfb, k4, pfb, k6—64 sts. Change to larger needles.

Begin Chart
Rnd 1 K30, sm, k4, work chart over 24 sts, k6.
Cont to work chart and St st (k every rnd) in this way through chart row 8, then rep rows 1–8 until piece measures 5½"/14cm from beg.
Next rnd K7 and place sts on scrap yarn for thumb, work in pat to end of rnd.
Next rnd Cast on 7 sts, work in pat to end—64 sts.
Cont in pats until piece measures 8½"/21.5cm from beg.

Shape Top
Dec rnd [Ssk, work in pat to 2 sts before marker, k2tog, sm] twice—4 sts dec'd.
Rep dec rnd every other rnd 8 times more—28 sts.
Next rnd Ssk, work in pat to 2 sts before marker, k2tog, sm, ssk, p2, [k2tog] 4 times, p2, k2tog—20 sts.
Place 10 front sts on one needle and 10 back sts on a 2nd needle.
Cut yarn leaving, a long tail, and graft rem sts closed using Kitchener st (see page 55).

Thumb
With larger needles, knit 7 sts from scrap yarn, pick up 1 st in corner, pick up and k 7 sts along cast-on of thumb opening, pick up 1 st in corner—16 sts. Divide sts over 3 needles (5 sts, 6 sts, 5 sts). Join and pm for beg of rnd. Work in St st until thumb measures 2½"/6.5cm.
Next rnd [K2tog] 8 times—8 sts.
Cut yarn, leaving long tail. Pull tail through rem sts, draw up, and secure.

FINISHING
Weave in ends. Block to measurements.

LEFT MITTEN
Work as for right mitten until rib is complete. At end of last rnd, remove beg of rnd marker, knit first st of next rnd,

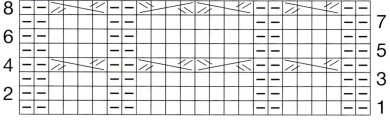
24 sts

STITCH KEY
☐ k on RS, p on WS
⊟ p on RS, k on WS
▱ 4-st RC
▱ 4-st LC

replace beg of rnd marker. Marker is now between 2 knit sts.
Next rnd K6, pfb, k4, pfb, k8, pfb, k4, pfb, k4, pm, k30—64 sts.
Change to larger needles.

Begin Chart
Rnd 1 K6, work chart over 24 sts, k4, sm, k30. Cont to work chart and St st in this way through chart row 8, then rep rows 1–8 until piece measures 5½"/14cm from beg.
Next rnd Work to last 7 sts, k7 and place sts on scrap yarn for thumb.
Next rnd Work to sts on holder, cast on 7 sts—64 sts.
Cont in pats until piece measures 8½"/21.5cm from beg.

Shape Top
Dec rnd [Ssk, work in pat to 2 sts before marker, k2tog, sm] twice—4 sts dec'd.
Rep dec rnd every other rnd 8 times more—28 sts.
Next rnd Ssk, p2, [k2tog] 4 times, p2, k2tog, sm, ssk, work in pat to last 2 sts, k2tog—20 sts.
Complete as for right mitten.•

Design Note
Throw a few cables into the mix. They may be a bit challenging, but the reward of stunning textures is well worth it.

Thick & Thin Striped Mittens

Easy

SIZE
Adult Woman.

MEASUREMENTS
Hand circumference 7¾"/19.5cm
Length 12"/30.5cm

MATERIALS
Yarn 🧶
1¾oz/50g, 117yd/107m of any DK weight wool/acrylic/nylon blend in Green Apple (MC) and Olive Green (CC)

Needles
• One pair size 4 (3.5mm) needles, *or size to obtain gauge*
• One set (5) size 4 (3.5mm) double-pointed needles (dpn)

Notions
• Stitch markers
• Scrap yarn

GAUGE
22 sts and 30 rnds to 4"/10cm over St st using size 4 (3.5mm) needles.
TAKE TIME TO CHECK YOUR GAUGE.

STITCH GLOSSARY
M1R Insert LH needle from back to front under the horizontal strand between the stitch just worked and the next st on LH needle, knit this loop through the front—1 st inc'd.
M1L Insert LH needle from front to back under the horizontal strand between the stitch just worked and the next st on LH needle, knit this loop through the back—1 st inc'd.

NOTE
Cuffs are worked flat and seamed, then hand is worked in the round from cuff to fingertips.

COLOR SEQUENCE A
Work 6 rows in CC, 4 rows in MC.
Rep these 10 rows for color sequence A.

COLOR SEQUENCE B
Work 8 rnds MC, 2 rnds CC, 14 rnds MC, 10 rnds CC, 6 rnds MC, 4 rnds CC—44 rnds.

LEFT MITTEN
Cuff
With straight needles and CC, cast on 43 sts.
Set-up row (WS) *P1, k3; rep from * to last 3 sts, p1, k1, p1.
Row 1 (RS) K4, *p1, k3; rep from * to last 3 sts, p1, k2.
Row 2 *P1, k3; rep from * to last 3 sts, p1, k1, p1.
Rep rows 1 and 2 for broken rib, AT THE SAME TIME, cont in color sequence A, beg with row 3 of sequence, until 40 rows in color sequence have been worked, end with a WS row in MC.
Place sts on scrap yarn and sew side seam.

Hand
Note Hand is worked in St st (k every rnd). Divide 43 sts over 4 dpn (10 sts, 11 sts, 11 sts, 11 sts), join to work in rnds, and pm for beg of rnd at seam.
Beg color sequence B, knit 2 rnds.

Thumb Gusset
Inc rnd 1 K3, pm, M1R, k1, M1L, pm, k to end—45 sts.
Rnd 2 Knit.
Rnd 3 K to marker, sm, M1R, k to next marker, M1L, sm, k to end—2 sts inc'd.
Rep last 2 rnds 5 times more—57 sts.
Next rnd K to marker, place 15 sts on scrap yarn, k to end—42 sts.
Cont in color sequence B until 44 rnds of color sequence have been worked—piece measures approx 10½"/26.5cm from beg.
Cont with A only to end of piece.

Shape Top
Dec rnd [K5, k2tog, pm] 6 times (last marker will be beg of rnd marker)—36 sts.
Work 2 rnds even.
Dec rnd [K to 2 sts before marker, k2tog] 6 times—6 sts dec'd.
Rep last 3 rnds 3 times more, then rep dec rnd once more—6 sts.
Cut yarn, pull tail through rem sts, draw up and secure.

Thumb
Place 6 sts from scrap yarn on each of 2 dpn, place rem 3 on 3rd dpn. With 3rd dpn and color in pat, pick up and k 3 sts along hand edge—18 sts. Divide sts evenly over 3 needles (6 sts on each needle).
With MC, knit 7 rnds. With CC, knit 7 rnds. Cont in CC to end.
Next rnd [K1, k2tog] 6 times—12 sts.
Knit 1 rnd.
Next rnd [K2tog] 6 times—6 sts.
Cut yarn, pull tail through rem sts, draw up and secure.

FINISHING
Weave in ends. Block to measurements.

RIGHT MITTEN
Work as for left mitten to thumb gusset.
Inc rnd 1 K to last 4 sts, pm, M1R, k1, M1L, pm, k3—45 sts.
Rnd 2 Knit.
Rnd 3 K to marker, sm, M1R, k to next marker, M1L, sm, k to end—2 sts inc'd.
Rep last 2 rnds 5 times more—57 sts.
Complete as for left mitten.•

Design Note 1
You can shape the top of a mitten in a number of ways. This pattern uses 6 decreases each decrease round.

Design Note 2
Increasing the length of a cuff and using a textured ribbing adds a lot of character to these striped mittens.

Cabled Mittens

Intermediate

SIZE
Adult Woman.

MEASUREMENTS
Hand circumference (unstretched)
6½"/16.5cm
Length 9"/23cm

MATERIALS
Yarn
• 3½oz/100g, 306yd/280m of any DK weight superwash wool in Red

Needles
• One set (4) size 4 (3.5mm) needles, *or size to obtain gauge*

Notions
• Cable needle (cn)
• Stitch marker
• Scrap yarn

GAUGE
22 sts and 30 rows to 4"/10cm over St st using size 4 (3.5mm) needles.
TAKE TIME TO CHECK YOUR GAUGE.

STITCH GLOSSARY
10-st RC Sl 5 sts to cn, hold to back, k5, k5 from cn.
10-st LC Sl 5 sts to cn, hold to front, k5, k5 from cn.
M1R Insert LH needle from back to front under the strand between last st worked and next st on LH needle. K into the front loop to twist the st.
M1L Insert LH needle from front to back under the strand between last st worked and next st on LH needle. K into the back loop to twist the st.
M1 p-st Insert needle from front to back under the strand between the last st worked and the next st on the LH needle. Purl into the back loop to twist the st.

CABLE PATTERN
(over 20 sts)
Rnds 1 and 2 Knit.
Rnd 3 10-st RC, 10-st LC.
Rnds 4–10 Knit.
Rep rnds 1–10 for cable pat.

RIGHT MITTEN
Cast on 51 sts and divide evenly over 3 dpn. Join, taking care not to twist sts, and pm for beg of rnd.
Rnd 1 *P1, k2; rep from * around.
Rep rnd 1 for p1, k2 rib for 3"/7.5cm.
Inc rnd *Pfb, k2; rep from * around, remove beg of rnd marker, p1, replace beg of rnd marker—68 sts. Marker is now between 2 purl sts.

Begin Cable Pattern
Rnd 1 [P1, k2, p1] twice, pm, work cable pat over 20 sts, pm, *p1, k2, p1; rep from * to end.
Rnd 2 Work in pats as established, working cable pat between markers.

Begin Thumb Gusset
Inc rnd 3 Work in pat to marker, sm, work cable pat over 20 sts, sm, [p1, k2, p1] twice, p1, pm for thumb, M1 p-st, k2, M1 p-st, pm for thumb, *p2, k2; rep from * to last st, p1—70 sts.
Rnd 4 Work even in pats.
Inc rnd 5 Work in pats to thumb marker, sm, M1 p-st, p1, k2, p1, M1 p-st, sm, work in pat to end—72 sts.
Rnd 6 Work even in pats.
Inc rnd 7 Work in pats to thumb marker, sm, M1R, work in pat to marker, M1L, sm, work in pat to end—2 sts inc'd.
Rnd 8 Work even in pats.
Rep rnds 7 and 8 four times more, working inc's into k2, p2 rib pat by working M1 p-st or M1R and M1L as established—82 sts in total, 16 thumbs sts between markers.
Rnd 17 Work in pats to thumb marker, place 16 thumb sts on scrap yarn, cast on 2 sts using backward loop cast-on, work in pat to end—68 sts.
Cont in pats as established until rows 1–10 of cable pat have been worked 4 times in total, then work rows 1–6 once more.

Shape Top
Dec rnd 1 P1, [k2, p2tog] 16 times, k2, sl next purl st to RH needle, remove marker, sl st back to LH needle and p2tog, replace beg of rnd marker—51 sts.
Rnds 2 and 3 *K2, p1; rep from * around.
Dec rnd 4 [K2tog, p1] 17 times—34 sts.
Rnds 5 and 6 *K1, p1; rep from * around.
Rnd 7 [K2tog] 17 times—17 sts.
Rnd 8 [K2tog] 8 times, k1—9 sts.
Cut yarn, leaving long tail. Pull tail through rem sts, draw up, and secure.

Thumb
Place 6 thumb sts on each of 2 dpn, place rem 4 sts on 3rd dpn. With RS facing, pick up and k 4 sts along hand edge, pm for beg of rnd—20 sts.
Rnd 1 K1, *p2, k2; rep from * to last 3 sts, p2, k1.
Rnds 2–11 Rep rnd 1.
Dec rnd 12 K1, [p2tog, k2] 4 times, p2tog, k1—15 sts.
Rnds 13 and 14 Work in pat as established.
Dec rnd 15 K1, [p1, k2tog] 4 times, p1, sl last st to RH needle, remove marker, replace st on LH needle and k2tog, replace marker—10 sts.
Rnd 16 *P1, k1; rep from * around.
Rnd 17 [K2tog] 5 times—5 sts.
Cut yarn, leaving long tail. Pull tail through rem sts, draw up, and secure.

FINISHING
Weave in ends. Block gently to measurements.

LEFT MITTEN
Work as for right mitten to begin thumb gusset.

Begin Thumb Gusset

Inc rnd 3 Work in pat to marker, sm, work cable pat over 20 sts, sm, [p1, k2, p1] 9 times, p1, pm for thumb, M1 p-st, k2, M1 p-st, pm for thumb, p1—70 sts.

Rnd 4 Work even in pats.

Inc rnd 5 Work in pats to thumb marker, sm, M1 p-st, p1, k2, p1, M1 p-st, sm, p1—72 sts.

Rnd 6 Work even in pats.

Inc rnd 7 Work in pats to thumb marker, sm, M1R, work in pat to marker, M1L, sm, p1—2 sts inc'd.

Rnd 8 Work even in pats. Rep rnds 7 and 8 four times more, working inc's into k2, p2 rib pat by working M1 p-st or M1R and M1L as established—82 sts in total, 16 thumbs sts between markers.

Rnd 17 Work in pats to thumb marker, place 16 thumb sts on scrap yarn, cast on 2 sts using backward loop cast on, p1—68 sts.

Complete as for right mitten.•

Design Note
Take your ribbing all the way from cuff to fingertip, adding in a wide cable for that extra touch.

Striped Mittens

Intermediate

SIZE
Adult Woman.

MEASUREMENTS
Hand circumference 8"/20.5cm
Length 7"/18cm

MATERIALS
Yarn
Any worsted weight nylon/acrylic blend, approx 3½oz/100g, 216yd/198m per skein
• 1 skein each in Blue (A) and Off-White (B)

Needles
• One set (5) each size 5 and 6 (3.75 and 4mm) double-pointed needles (dpn), *or size to obtain gauge*

Notions
• Stitch markers
• Stitch holders

GAUGE
16 sts and 26 rnds to 4"/10cm over St st using larger needles.
TAKE TIME TO CHECK YOUR GAUGE.

STITCH GLOSSARY
M1R Insert LH needle from back to front under the horizontal strand between the stitch just worked and the next st on LH needle, knit this loop through the front—1 st inc'd.
M1L Insert LH needle from front to back under the horizontal strand between the stitch just worked and the next st on LH needle, knit this loop through the back—1 st inc'd.

NOTE
When changing color in stripe pats, carry yarn not in use along inside, twisting over working yarn.

WIDE STRIPE PATTERN
With A, knit 3 rnds; with B, knit 3 rnds.
Rep these 6 rnds for wide stripe pat.

NARROW STRIPE PATTERN
With A, knit 1 rnd; with B, knit 1 rnd.
Rep these 2 rnds for narrow stripe pat.

RIGHT MITTEN
With smaller dpn and B, cast on 32 sts. Divide sts evenly over 4 needles. Join, taking care not to twist sts, and pm for beg of rnd. Knit 1 rnd. Work in stripes and rib as foll:
Rnd 1 With A, knit.
Rnds 2 and 3 With A, *k2, p2; rep from * around.
Rnd 4 With B, knit.
Rnds 5 and 6 With B, *k2, p2; rep from * around.
Rep rnds 1–6 twice more. Piece measures approx 2½"/6.5cm from beg. Change to larger dpn.

Begin Thumb Gusset
Beg with 3 rnds A, work in wide stripe pat as foll:
Rnd 1 Knit.
Rnd 2 K2, pm, M1R, pm, k to end—33 sts.
Rnd 3 Knit.
Rnd 4 K2, sm, M1R, k to marker, M1L, sm, k to end—2 sts inc'd.
Rnds 5 and 6 Knit.
Rep rnds 4–6 four times more—43 sts total, 11 between markers.
Next rnd K2, place 11 sts for thumb on st holder (remove thumb markers), k14, pm, k to end—32 sts.
Cont in St st (k every rnd) and wide stripe pat until piece measures approx 7½"/19cm from beg, end with 3 rnds A.

Shape Top
Dec rnd 1 With B, [k2, ssk, k to 4 sts before marker, k2tog, k2, sm] twice—4 sts dec'd.
Cont in narrow stripe pat, work as foll:
Rnds 2 and 3 Knit.
Working in narrow stripe pat, rep rnds 1–3 once—24 sts.
Cont with A only, rep rnds 1 and 2 once more, then rnd 1 twice more—12 sts.
Place 6 front sts on one needle and 6 back sts on a 2nd needle.
Cut yarn leaving a long tail and graft rem sts closed using Kitchener st (see page 48).

Thumb
With larger dpn and A, pick up and k 2 sts along hand edge, knit 11 thumb sts, pick up and k 3 sts from hand edge, pm—16 sts. Divide sts over 3 needles (5 sts, 6 sts, 5 sts).
Cont in narrow stripe pat, work as foll:
Dec rnd 1 K1, ssk, k to last 3 sts, k2tog, k1—14 sts.
Work in St st until thumb measures 1½"/4cm, end with a B stripe.
Cont with A only to end.
Next dec rnd [K2tog] 7 times—7 sts.
Next rnd Knit.
Next dec rnd [K2tog] 3 times, k1—4 sts.
Cut yarn, pull tail through rem sts, draw up and secure.

FINISHING
Weave in ends. Block lightly to measurements.

LEFT MITTEN

Work as for right mitten to thumb gusset.

Begin Thumb Gusset
Rnd 1 Knit.
Rnd 2 K14, pm, M1R, pm, k to end—33 sts.
Rnd 3 Knit.
Rnd 4 K14, sm, M1R, k to marker, M1L, sm, k to end—2 sts inc'd.
Rnds 5–6 Knit.
Rep rnds 4–6 four times more—43 sts total, 11 between markers.
Next rnd K14, place 11 sts for thumb on st holder, k2, pm, k to end—32 sts.
Complete as for right mitten.•

Design Note
Earn your stripes by varying their width. It'll add a fun dimension to the overall pattern.

Long Cabled Mittens

Intermediate

SIZE
Adult Woman.

MEASUREMENTS
Hand circumference 8"/20.5cm
Length 15"/38cm

MATERIALS
Yarn
• 3½oz/100g, 274yd/250m of any DK weight acrylic in Red

Needles
• One set (4) each size 6 and 8 (4 and 5mm) double-pointed needles (dpn), *or size to obtain gauge*

Notions
• Cable needle (cn)
• Stitch markers
• Scrap yarn

GAUGE
16 sts and 30 rnds to 4"/10cm over cable twist pat using larger needles.
TAKE TIME TO CHECK YOUR GAUGE.

STITCH GLOSSARY
2-st LC Sl 1 st to cn and hold to front, k1, k1 from cn.
4-st LC Sl 2 sts to cn and hold to front, k2, k2 from cn.
4-st dec LC Sl 2 sts to cn and hold to front, k2tog, k2tog from cn—2 sts dec'd.
M1 Make 1 knit stitch by inserting tip of LH needle from front to back under strand between last stitch worked and next stitch; knit into back loop—1 st inc'd.
M1 p-st Make 1 purl stitch by inserting tip of LH needle from back to front under strand between last stitch worked and next stitch; purl into front loop—1 st inc'd.

CABLE TWIST PATTERN
(multiple of 8 sts)
Rnd 1 *4-st LC, p4; rep from * around.
Rnds 2 and 3 *K4, p4; rep from * around.
Rep rnds 1–3 for cable twist pat.

MITTENS
With larger dpn, cast on 48 sts, dividing evenly over 3 dpn. Join, taking care not to twist sts, and pm for beg of rnd.

Begin Cable Twist Pattern
Rnd 1 Work 8-st rep of cable twist pat 6 times around.
Cont to work cable twist pat in this way until piece measures 5½"/14cm from beg, end with a rnd 1.
Dec rnd *K4, p1, p2tog, p1; rep from * around—42 sts.
Work 8 rnds even in pat, working 3 purl sts between cable ribs.
Dec rnd *4-st dec LC, p3, [4-st LC, p3] twice; rep from * once more—38 sts.
Work 3 rnds even in pat, working 2-st LC over dec'd cables.

Begin Thumb Gusset
Inc rnd 1 [M1, k1] twice, pm, work to end of rnd—40 sts.
Rnd 2 K1, p2, k1, work to end of rnd.
Rnd 3 K1, M1, p2, M1, k1, work to end of rnd—42 sts.
Rnd 4 K1, p2, k1, M1, p1, k1, work to end of rnd—43 sts.
Rnd 5 K1, M1 p-st, p2, k1, p2, M1 p-st, k1, work to end of rnd—45 sts.
Rnds 6 and 7 Work even in pats.
Rnd 8 K1, M1 p-st, p3, k1, p3, M1 p-st, k1, work to end of rnd—47 sts.
Rnds 9 and 10 Work even in pats.
Rnd 11 K1, M1 p-st, p4, k1, p4, M1 p-st, k1, work to end of rnd—49 sts.
Rnd 12 Work even in pats.
Next rnd Place next 13 sts on scrap yarn for thumb, cast on 6 sts, work to end of rnd—42 sts.
Next rnd Work (p2, k2, p2) over cast-on sts, work in pats to end.
Cont in pats over all sts, working a 2-st LC over 2 knit sts of cast-on sts on each rnd 1 of cable twist pat, until piece measures 14½"/37cm from beg, end with a rnd 3 of pat.

Shape Top
Dec rnd P2tog, 2-st LC, p2tog, p1, p2tog, [4-st dec LC, p1, p2tog] twice, 2-st LC, p1, p2tog, [4-st dec LC, p1, p2tog] twice—26 sts.
Work 2 rnds even in pats.
Dec rnd P1, 2-st LC, p1, p2tog, [2-st LC, p2tog] 5 times—20 sts.
Dec rnd [K2tog] 10 times.
Cut yarn, leaving long tail. Pull tail through rem sts, draw up, and secure.

Thumb
Place 13 sts on hold for thumb on smaller dpn. Pick up and k 7 sts from edge of hand—20 sts. Divide sts over 3 dpn (7 sts, 7 sts, 6 sts), join, and pm for beg of rnd. Rnd begins at first st from held sts.
Rnds 1–3 [K1, p5] twice, k1, p7.
Rnd 4 Work in pat, dec 1 st in each purl section—17 sts.
Rnds 5–7 Work even.
Rnd 8 Rep rnd 4—14 sts.
Rnds 9–11 Work even.
Rnd 12 Rep rnd 4—11 sts.
Rnds 13–15 Work even.
Rnd 16 Dec 5 sts evenly around—6 sts.
Cut yarn, leaving long tail. Pull tail through rem sts, draw up, and secure.

FINISHING
Weave in ends. Block lightly to measurements.
Rep from beg for 2nd mitten. •

Design Note
While cuffs tend to be only a couple of inches long, you can make them longer for extra warmth.

Heart-Motif Mittens

Intermediate

SIZE
Adult Woman.

MEASUREMENTS
Hand circumference 8"/20.5cm
Length 7½"/19cm

MATERIALS
Yarn
• 3½oz/100g, 224yd/205m of any DK weight merino wool Blue (A) and Red (B)

Needles
• One set (5) each size 2 and 3 (2.75 and 3.25mm) double-pointed needles (dpn), *or size to obtain gauge*
• One pair size 3 (3.25mm) needles

Notions
• Stitch markers
• Stitch holders

GAUGE
22 sts and 32 rnds/rows to 4"/10cm over St st using larger needles.
TAKE TIME TO CHECK YOUR GAUGE.

STITCH GLOSSARY
M1R Insert LH needle from back to front under the horizontal strand between the stitch just worked and the next st on LH needle, knit this loop through the front—1 st inc'd.
M1L Insert LH needle from front to back under the horizontal strand between the stitch just worked and the next st on LH needle, knit this loop through the back—1 st inc'd.
M1 p-st Insert needle from front to back under the horizontal strand between the last st worked and the next st on the LH needle. Purl into the back loop to twist the stitch—1 st inc'd.

NOTES
1) Mittens are worked in the round to the heart motif, then worked back and forth while knitting the 18 rows of the heart motif, then rejoined and worked in the round to the end of the mitten.
2) When changing colors, twist yarns on WS to prevent holes in work.

RIGHT MITTEN
With smaller dpn and B, cast on 44 sts. Divide sts evenly over 4 needles (11 sts on each needle). Join, taking care not to twist sts, and pm for beg of rnd. Cut B. Join A.
Rnd 1 Knit.
Rnd 2 *K2, p2; rep from * around.
Rep rnd 2 for k2, p2 rib for 2½"/6.5cm. Change to larger dpn.

Begin Thumb Gusset
Rnd 1 Knit.
Rnd 2 K11, M1R, k11, pm, M1R, pm, k to end—46 sts.
Rnd 3 Knit.
Rnd 4 K to marker, sm, M1R, work to marker, M1L, sm, k to end—2 sts inc'd.
Rnds 5 and 6 Knit.
Rep rnds 4–6 five times more—58 sts total, 13 sts between markers.
Next rnd K to marker, drop marker, place 13 sts for thumb on st holder, sm, k to end—45 sts.

Begin Chart
Note Chart is worked in St st.
Change to straight needles and work next 18 rows back and forth as foll:
Row 1 (RS) Work chart over 23 sts, sm, k to end.
Row 2 P to marker, sm, work chart to end.
Cont to work chart in this way through row 18. Cut B.
Divide sts again over 4 dpn and join to work in rounds with A only to end of mitten as foll:
Knit 2 rnds.

Shape Top
Dec rnd 1 [K2, ssk, k to 4 sts before marker, k2tog, k2] twice—4 sts dec'd.
Rnds 2 and 3 Knit.
Rep rnd 1–3 once more, then rep rnds 1 and 2 only 3 times more—25 sts.
Next dec rnd K2, ssk, k1, k2tog, k2, k2tog, k4, ssk, k4, k2tog, k2—20 sts.
Next dec rnd [K2, ssk, k2, k2tog, k2] twice—16 sts.
Next dec rnd [K2, ssk, k2tog, k2] twice—12 sts.
Place 6 front sts on one needle and 6 back sts on a 2nd needle.
Cut yarn, leaving a long tail, and graft rem sts closed using Kitchener st (see page 55).

Thumb
With larger dpn and A, pick up and k 2 sts along hand edge, k 13 thumb sts, pick up and k 3 sts from hand edge—18 sts.
Divide sts evenly over 3 needles (6 sts on each needle).
Knit 1 rnd.
Next dec rnd K1, ssk, k to last 3 sts, k2tog, k1—16 sts.
Work even in St st until thumb measures

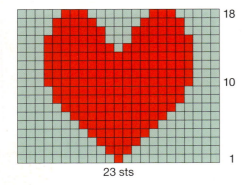

23 sts

COLOR KEY
☐ Blue (A)
■ Red (B)

1½"/4cm, end with a WS row.
Next dec rnd [K2tog] 8 times—8 sts.
Next rnd Knit.
Next dec rnd [K2tog] 4 times—4 sts.
Cut yarn, pull tail through rem sts, draw up and secure.

FINISHING
Use tail to sew thumb seam.
Sew side seam.
Weave in ends. Block lightly to measurements.

LEFT MITTEN
Work as for right mitten to thumb gusset.

Begin Thumb Gusset
Rnd 1 Knit.
Rnd 2 K22, pm, M1R, pm, k11, M1R, k11—46 sts.
Rnd 3 Knit.
Rnd 4 Work to marker, sm, M1R, work to marker, M1L, sm, work to end—2 sts inc'd.
Rnds 5 and 6 Knit.
Rep rnds 4–6 five times more—58 sts total, 13 sts between markers.
Next rnd K to marker, place 13 sts for thumb on st holder, pm, k to end—45 sts.

Begin Chart
Note Chart is worked in St st.
Change to straight needles and work next 18 rows back and forth as foll:
Row 1 K to marker, sm, work chart over 23 sts.
Complete as for right mitten. •

Design Note
If intarsia isn't your thing, you can work the entire mitten in the round with the main color and then use duplicate stitch (see page 56) to add the heart—or any other motif you would like.

Wave-Patterned Mittens

Easy

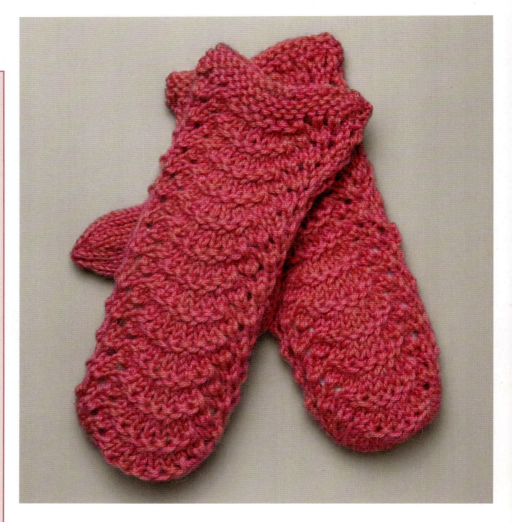

SIZE
Adult Woman.

MEASUREMENTS
Hand circumference 8"/20.5cm
Length 8½"/21.5cm

MATERIALS
Yarn
• 1¾oz/50g, 115yd/105m of any DK weight wool/mohair/alpaca blend in Raspberry

Needles
• One pair size 6 (4mm) needles, *or size to obtain gauge*
• One set (4) size 6 (4mm) double-pointed needles (dpn)

Notions
• Stitch marker
• Scrap yarn

GAUGE
19 sts and 22 rows to 4"/10cm over wave st using size 6 (4mm) needles.
TAKE TIME TO CHECK YOUR GAUGE.

WAVE STITCH
Row 1 (RS) Knit.
Row 2 Purl.
Row 3 Knit.
Row 4 P1, [yo, p1] 3 times, [k2tog] 6 times, [yo, p1] 6 times, [k2tog] 6 times, [yo, p1] 3 times.
Rep rows 1–4 for wave st.

NOTE
Mittens are worked back and forth in rows from tip to cuff.

LEFT MITTEN
Cast on 37 sts.
Work rows 1–4 of wave st 7 times, then rep row 1 once more.

Thumb Opening
Next row (WS) P12, sl next 6 sts to scrap yarn, turn work to RS and cast on 6 sts, turn work to WS and p rem 19 sts.
Cont in wave pat over 37 sts until rows 1–4 have been worked 13 times in total.
Knit 4 rows.
Bind off knitwise.

Thumb
With RS facing and dpn, pick up and k 6 sts along cast-on edge of thumb opening, pick up and k 2 sts along side edge, sl 6 sts from holder to dpn and k6, pick up and k 2 sts along opposite side edge—16 sts.
Divide sts over 3 needles (5 sts, 6 sts, 5 sts) and pm for beg of rnd.
Knit 12 rnds.
Dec rnd [K2tog] 8 times—8 sts.
Knit 1 rnd.
Dec rnd [K2tog] 4 times—4 sts.
Cut yarn and pull through rem sts, draw up and secure.
Block lightly. Sew side and top seam.

RIGHT MITTEN
Work as for left mitten to thumb opening.
Next row P19, sl next 6 sts to scrap yarn, turn work to RS and cast on 6 sts, turn work to WS and p rem 12 sts.
Complete as for left mitten.•

Design Note
Try this fun experiment: knit your mittens upside down by working them in rows from tip to cuff.

Open Up More Possibilities

When you need a little extra warmth but want to keep your fingers free, fingerless mittens are just the thing. They are constructed similarly to traditional mittens, but they are not closed at the fingers or thumbs. Fingerless mittens go by a few names—mitts, wristers, wristlets, hand warmers—but no matter what you call them, they're fun to knit and practical to wear.

Slip Stitch Mitts

Easy

MEASUREMENTS
Hand circumference 7½"/19cm
Length 10¼"/26cm

MATERIALS
Yarn (4)
• 3½oz/100g, 244yd/222m of any worsted weight superwash wool in Gray (A)
• 1¾oz/50g, 122yd/111m of any worsted weight superwash wool in Yellow (B)

Needles
• One pair size 6 (4mm) needles, *or size to obtain gauge*
• One set (5) size 6 (4mm) double-pointed needles (dpn)

Notions
• Stitch markers
• Scrap yarn

GAUGE
22 sts and 31 rows to 4"/10cm in St st using size 6 (4mm) needles.
TAKE TIME TO CHECK YOUR GAUGE.

STITCH GLOSSARY
M1R Insert LH needle from back to front under the horizontal strand between the stitch just worked and the next st on LH needle, knit this loop through the front—1 st inc'd.
M1L Insert LH needle from front to back under the horizontal strand between the stitch just worked and the next st on LH needle, knit this loop through the back—1 st inc'd.

K1, P1 RIBBING
(over an odd number of sts in rows)
Row 1 *K1, p1; rep from * to last st, k1.
Row 2 *P1, k1; rep from * to last st, p1.
Rep rows 1 and 2 for k1, p1 rib.

K1, P1 RIBBING
(over an even number of sts in rnds)
Rnd 1 *K1, p1; rep from * to end of rnd.
Rep rnd 1 for k1, p1 rib.

TEXTURED STRIPE PATTERN
(over an odd number of sts in rows)
Row 1 (RS) With B, k1, *sl 1 wyif, k1; rep from * to end.
Row 2 With B, purl.
Row 3 With A, k2, *sl 1 wyif, k1; rep from * to last st, k1.
Row 4 With A, purl.
Row 5 With A, knit.
Row 6 With A, purl.
Rows 7–9 Rep rows 1–3.
Row 10 With A, purl.

RIGHT MITT
With straight needles and A, cast on 43 sts. Work 2 rows in k1, p1 rib, end with a WS row. Beg with a knit (RS) row, work in St st (k on RS, p on WS) until piece from beg measures 6¼"/16cm from beg, end with a WS row.

Begin Thumb Gusset
Next row (RS) K22, pm, M1R, k1, M1L, pm, k to end—45 sts.
Next row Purl.
Next row K22, sm, M1R, k to marker, M1L, sm, k to end—47 sts.
Next row Purl.
Rep last 2 rows 5 times more—15 sts between markers.
Next row (RS) K22, remove marker, place next 15 sts on scrap yarn, remove 2nd marker, cast on 1 st and k to end—43 sts.
Work 5 rows even in St st.
Work rows 1–10 of textured stripe pat.
With MC, work 1 row in k1, p1 ribbing.
Bind off in rib.

Thumb
Place 15 thumb sts on dpn and divide over 4 dpn.
Rnd 1 Pick up and k 1 st at base of thumb, k15, join and pm for beg of rnd—16 sts.
Knit 3 rnds. Work 1 rnd in k1, p1 rib.
Bind off in rib.

FINISHING
Sew side seam.
Weave in ends. Block to measurements.

LEFT MITT
Work as for right mitt to thumb gusset.
Next row (RS) K20, pm, M1R, k1, M1L, pm, k to end—45 sts.
Complete to correspond to right mitt. ●

Design Note
Step up your stripes! These fingerless gloves use a simple slip-stitch pattern to create a texture that's as fun to knit as it is to look at.

Shell Rib Wristlets

Easy

SIZE
Will stretch to fit most.

MEASUREMENTS
Circumference (unstretched) 6"/15cm
Length 9"/23cm

MATERIALS
Yarn
• 3½oz/100g, 228yd/208m of any DK weight wool in Blue

Needles
• One pair size 6 (4mm) needles, *or size to obtain gauge*

GAUGE
21 sts and 30 rows to 4"/10cm over shell rib using size 6 (4mm) needles.
TAKE TIME TO CHECK YOUR GAUGE.

SHELL RIB
(multiple of 7 sts plus 2)
Row 1 (WS) P2, *k1, [yo, k1] 4 times, p2; rep from * to end—multiple is now 11 sts plus 2.
Row 2 K2, *p1, [k1, p1] 4 times, k2; rep from * to end.
Row 3 P2, *k1, p1, ssk, k1, k2tog, p1, k1, p2; rep from * to end.
Row 4 K2, *p1, k1, p3tog, k1, p1, k2; rep from * to end—multiple is back to 7 sts plus 2.
Rep rows 1–4 for shell rib.

WRISTLET
Cast on 30 sts. Work in shell rib for 9"/23cm, end with a WS row. Bind off loosely.

FINISHING
Fold wristlet in half lengthwise. Beg at lower edge, sew side seam for 6½"/16.5cm, leave next 1"/2.5cm unsewn for thumb opening, sew rem 1½"/4cm to close wristlet.
Weave in ends. Block lightly.•

Design Note
Worked in rows and forgoing any sort of thumb, these fingerless mittens are as simple as can be while remaining eye-catching and fun to knit.

Ribbed Fingerless Mitts

Easy

SIZES
Small/Medium (Large/X-Large).
Shown in Small/Medium.

MEASUREMENTS
Circumference 6¾ (7½)"/17 (19)cm*
*Ribbing will stretch to fit
Length (with cuff unfolded)
11¼"/28.5cm

MATERIALS
Yarn
- 4.16oz/118g, 225yd/206m of any worsted weight superwash wool in Chartreuse (MC) and Lavender (CC)

Needles
- One pair each size 7 and 8 (4.5 and 5mm) needles, *or size to obtain gauge*
- One set (4) size 7 (4.5mm) double-pointed needles (dpn)

Notions
- Stitch marker

GAUGE
20 sts and 22 rows to 4"/10cm over k2, p2 rib (slightly stretched) using smaller needles.
TAKE TIME TO CHECK YOUR GAUGE.

P2, K2 RIB
(multiple of 4 sts plus 2)
Row 1 (RS of cuff, WS of main body)
P2, *k2, p2; rep from * to end.
Row 2 K2, *p2, k2; rep from * to end.
Rep rows 1 and 2 for k2, p2 rib.

CUFF
With larger needles and CC, cast on 34 (38) sts loosely. Purl 1 row on WS. Change to MC.
Beg with a RS row of cuff, work in k2, p2 rib until piece measures 3¾"/9.5cm from beg.

MAIN BODY
Change to smaller needles and cont in rib until piece measures 11"/28cm from beg, end with a RS row.
Change to CC and purl 1 row on WS. Bind off loosely in rib.
Work 2nd mitt in same way.

FINISHING
Sew side seams as foll:
With RS of cuff facing (with p2 at edges), beg at cast-on edge and using mattress st, sew cuff seam for 3¾"/9.5cm, turn piece inside out so that edge sts are now k2 and cont seaming from
RS of main body for 4½ (4)"/11.5 (10)cm. Skip 1½ (2)"/4 (5)cm for thumb opening and sew rem 1½"/4cm to end of piece.

Thumb
With RS facing, dpn and MC, pick up and k 12 (16) sts evenly around thumb opening. Join to work in rnds and pm to mark beg of rnd.
Next rnd *K2, p2; rep from * around.
Rep last rnd for k2, p2 rib for 5 rnds more.
Cut MC, join CC and knit 1 rnd.
Bind off loosely.•

Design Note 1
These mitts are worked in rows with no thumb gusset. Simply seam the sides, leaving an opening for the thumb, and then pick up and knit the thumb in the round.

Design Note 2
Use a contrasting color at the cuff and top for a sophisticated touch of colorplay.

Meow Meow Mitts

●●● Intermediate

SIZE
Adult woman.

MEASUREMENTS
Hand circumference 7½"/19cm
Length 8"/20.5cm

MATERIALS
Yarn
Any worsted weight acrylic/wool blend, approx 3oz/85g skeins, 197yd/180m per skein
• 1 skein each in Blue (A) and White (B)

Needles
• One pair each size 6 and 7 (4 and 4.5mm) needles, *or size to obtain gauge*
• Three size 6 (4mm) double-pointed needles (dpn)

Notions
• Stitch markers
• Stitch holders
• Tapestry needle

GAUGE
18 sts and 23 rows to 4"/10cm over St st using larger needles.
TAKE TIME TO CHECK YOUR GAUGE.

RIGHT MITT
With smaller needles and A, cast on 36 sts.
Row 1 *K1, p1; rep from * to end.
Rep row 1 for k1, p1 rib for 2¼"/5.5cm. Change to larger needles.
*With B, work 2 rows in St st (k on RS, p on WS), with A, work 2 rows in St st. Rep from * for 4-row stripe pat, *AT THE SAME TIME,* when 6 rows from cuff have been worked, shape thumb gusset as foll:
Next inc row (RS) K17, pm, [kfb] twice, pm, k17—38 sts.
Purl 1 row.
Inc row (RS) K to marker, sm, kfb, k to 1 st before next marker, kfb, sm, k to end—2 sts inc'd.
Cont in stripe pat, rep inc row every other row 5 times more—16 sts between markers.
Purl 1 row.
Next row K to marker, remove marker, k1, place next 14 thumb sts on st holder, cast on 1 st, k1, remove marker, k to end—37 sts on needle.
Purl 1 row.

Begin Chart 1
Note Work chart in St st. Discontinue stripe pat, work all sts outside of chart in St st with A only.
Row 1 With A, k3; work 11 sts of chart 1; with A, k to end.
Cont to work chart in this way through row 14. With A, work 3 rows in St st.
Next row (WS) With A, purl, dec'ing 5 sts evenly across—32 sts.
Change to smaller needles. Work 1 row in k1, p1 rib. Bind off in rib on WS, leaving a long tail for sewing.

Thumb
Divide 14 sts over 2 dpn for ease in working.
Join B ready to work a RS row.
Row 1 (RS) K2tog, k10, ssk—12 sts.
Purl 1 row.
With A, work 2 rows in St st.
With B, work 2 rows in St st.
With A, work 1 row in k1, p1 rib. Bind off in rib on WS, leaving tail for sewing.

LEFT MITT
Work as for right mitt to Begin Chart.

Begin Chart 2
Row 1 (RS) With A, k23; work chart 2 over 11 sts; with A, k3.
Complete as for right mitt.

FINISHING
With single ply of A, using chart as guide, work French knots for eyes and straight sts for whiskers (see page 56), tacking at center where whiskers cross.

Tail (make 2)
With dpn and B, work I-cord as foll: Cast on 3 sts. *Knit one row. Without turning work, slide sts back to opposite end of needle to work next row from RS. Pull yarn tightly from the end of the row. Rep from * until I-cord measures 3"/7.5cm. Bind off. Attach one end as indicated in chart, attach opposite end approx 5 rows below and 6–7 sts over, using photo as guide.
Sew side seams. Sew thumb seams. Weave in ends.•

KEY
■ Blue (A)
☐ White (B)
⊚ french knot
⧄ straight stitch
● = tail placement

CHART 1 — 11 sts
CHART 2 — 11 sts

Design Note
Make your knits stand out—literally—by adding 3D embellishments. The I-cord used here as a tail adds whimsy and charm.

Ring Around the Wristers

Easy

MEASUREMENTS
Hand circumference 8"/20.5cm
Length 8"/20.5cm

MATERIALS
Yarn
- 3½oz/100g, 263yd/240m of any DK weight wool in Pink.

Needles
- One set (4) size 5 (3.75mm) double-pointed needles (dpn), *or size to obtain gauge*

Notions
- Removable stitch markers
- Scrap yarn

GAUGE
22 sts and 32 rnds to 4"/10cm over St st using size 5 (3.75mm) needles.
TAKE TIME TO CHECK YOUR GAUGE.

STITCH GLOSSARY
M1R Insert LH needle from back to front under the strand between last st worked and next st on LH needle. K into the front loop to twist the st.
M1L Insert LH needle from front to back under the strand between last st worked and next st on LH needle. K into the back loop to twist the st.
M1 p-st Insert needle from front to back under the strand between the last st worked and the next st on the LH needle. Purl into the back loop to twist the st.

K2, P2 RIBBING
(over a multiple of 4 sts)
Rnd 1 *K2, p2; rep from * around.
Rep rnd 1 for k2, p2 rib.

WRISTER
With dpn, cast on 44 sts and divide sts over 3 dpn (16 sts, 14 sts, 14 sts). Join, taking care not to twist sts, and pm for beg of rnd.
Knit 3 rnds.
Work 3 rnds in k2, p2 rib.
Work in St st (k every rnd) until piece measures 3¼"/8.5cm from beg.
Purl 1 rnd, *knit 3 rnds, purl 3 rnds, knit 3 rnds, purl 1 rnd.
Rep from * twice more.

Begin Thumb Gusset
Cont in St st (k every rnd) and work as foll:
Inc rnd 1 K1, M1R, k1, M1L, pm, k to end of rnd.
Rnd 2 Knit.
Inc rnd 3 K1, M1R, k to marker, M1L, sm, k to end of rnd.
Rnd 4 Purl.
Inc rnd 5 P1, M1 p-st, p to marker, M1 p-st, sm, p to end of rnd.
Rnd 6 Purl.
Rnd 7 Rep inc rnd 3.
Rnd 8 Knit.
Rnd 9 Rep inc rnd 3.
Rnd 10 Purl.
Rnd 11 Rep inc rnd 3.
Rnd 12 Knit.
Rnd 13 Rep inc rnd 3.
Rnd 14 Knit.
Next rnd K1, place next 15 sts on scrap yarn for thumb, cast on 3 sts, k to end of rnd—46 sts.

Top of Hand
Knit 6 rnds.
Next rnd K2tog, k1, *p2, k2; rep from * around to last 3 sts, p2tog, p1—44 sts.
Work 2 rnds in k2, p2 rib. Bind off in rib.

Thumb
Place 15 sts on hold for the thumb onto dpn, then pick up and k 3 in cast-on sts—18 sts. Divide sts evenly over 3 dpn.
Next 2 rnds *K1, p1; rep from * to end.
Bind off in pat.

FINISHING
Weave in ends. Block lightly to measurements.
Rep from beg for 2nd wrister.•

Design Note
While many textures run the length of a mitten, this one circles the wrist and hand for a unique spin.

Leaf Rib Wristers

Easy

SIZE
Will stretch to fit most.

MEASUREMENTS
Circumference (unstretched)
6¾"/17cm
Length 10"/25.5cm

MATERIALS
Yarn
• 3½oz/100g, 270yd/247m of any DK weight wool/viscose blend in Variegated Blue

Needles
• One pair size 4 (3.5mm) needles, *or size to obtain gauge*

GAUGE
20 sts and 28 rows to 4"/10cm over leaf rib using size 4 (3.5mm) needles.
TAKE TIME TO CHECK YOUR GAUGE.

LEAF RIB
(multiple of 6 sts plus 4)
Rows 1 and 3 (WS) Purl.
Row 2 (RS) K2, *k3, yo, SK2P, yo; rep from *, to last 2 sts, k2.
Row 4 K2, *yo, SK2P, yo, k3; rep from * to last 2 sts, k2.
Rep rows 1–4 for leaf rib.

WRISTER
Cast on 34 sts using picot cast-on as foll: *Cast on 6 sts, bind off 2 sts; rep from *, end cast on 2 sts.
Knit 1 row, purl 1 row, knit 1 row.
Work in leaf rib until piece measures 10"/25.5cm from beg, end with a WS row. Bind off loosely.

FINISHING
Fold wrister in half lengthwise. Beg at lower edge, sew side seam for 7½"/19cm, leave next 1"/2.5cm unsewn for thumb opening, sew rem 1½"/4cm to close wrister.
Weave in ends. Block lightly.•

Design Note
There are many different types of cast-ons. This project calls for a picot cast-on, which is decorative and ties in well with the overall pattern.

Cuffed Wristers

Easy

SIZE
Adult Man.

MEASUREMENTS
Hand circumference 8"/20.5cm
Length (with rib folded) 9"/23cm

MATERIALS
Yarn (3)
• 3½oz/100g, 220yd/200m of any DK weight alpaca in Blue

Needles
• One set (5) size 3 (3.25mm) double-pointed needles (dpn), *or size to obtain gauge*

Notions
• Stitch marker

GAUGE
25 sts and 30 rnds to 4"/10cm over k4, p1 rib using size 3 (3.25mm) needles.
TAKE TIME TO CHECK YOUR GAUGE.

WRISTER
Cast on 50 sts and divide over 4 dpn. Join, taking care not to twist sts, and pm for beg of rnd.
Rnd 1 *K1, p1; rep from * around.
Rep rnd 1 for k1, p1 rib for 16 rnds more.
Rnds 18 and 19 Knit.
Rnd 20 K2, p1, *k4, p1; rep from * to last 2 sts, k2.
Rep rnd 20 for k4, p1 rib until piece measures 4½"/11.5cm from beg.
Turn and work back and forth in rows for thumb opening as foll:
Next row (WS) P1 tbl, work in rib as established to end.
Next row (RS) Work in rib as established. Cont to work back and forth in rib for 9 rows more.
Next row (RS) K1 tbl, work in rib to last st, k last st tbl. Do *not* turn, join and cont to work in rnds as foll:
Next rnd Rep rnd 20.
Cont in k4, p1 rib as established until piece measures 2½"/6.5cm from thumb opening. Knit 2 rnds.
Work 17 rnds in k1, p1 rib. Bind off in rib.

FINISHING
Weave in ends. Block lightly.
Fold k1, p1 rib at top of glove to RS to wear.
Rep from beg for 2nd wrister.•

Design Note
Mix things up by putting a foldable cuff at the top of your wristers.

Out of Line Mitts

Intermediate

SIZE
Will stretch to fit most.

MEASUREMENTS
Hand circumference 7¼"/18.5cm
Length 7½"/19cm

MATERIALS
Yarn ①
• 3½oz/100g, 416yd/380m of any fingering weight wool/nylon/silk blend in Gray

Needles
• One pair each size 1 and 2 (2.25 and 2.75mm) needles, *or size to obtain gauge*
• One set (4) size 1 (2.25mm) double-pointed needles (dpn)

Notions
• Scrap yarn
• Removable stitch markers

GAUGE
40 sts and 40 rows to 4"/10cm over k2, p2 rib, slightly stretched, using larger needles.
TAKE TIME TO CHECK YOUR GAUGE.

STITCH GLOSSARY
M1 open-knit With LH needle, lift yo strand by inserting needle from front to back and k tbl in this strand.
M1 open-purl With LH needle, lift yo strand by inserting needle from front to back and p tbl in this strand.
M1R knitwise Lift the horizontal strand between st just knit and next st and k tbl in this strand to M1R knitwise.

RIGHT MITT
With larger needles, cast on 74 sts.
Row 1 (RS) K1 (selvage st), *p2, k2; rep from * to last st, k1 (selvage st).
Row 2 (WS) P1 (selvage st), *p2, k2; rep from * to last st, p1 (selvage st).
Rep rows 1 and 2 for k2, p2 rib for a total of 30 rows.

Thumb Placement
Next row (RS) Work 35 sts, pm, k2, pm, work 37 sts.
Note These 2 placed markers (use a different color for the slant detail markers) will be referred to after the slant detail has been set up over 4 rows.
Next row (WS) Work even in rib.
Piece measures approx 3¼"/8cm from beg (with mitt slightly stretched to match the gauge).

Left Slant Detail
Slant row 1 (RS) Rib 7, yo, pm, k1, SKP, rib to end.
Slant row 2 (WS) *Rib to 3 sts before slant marker, p2tog tbl, p1, sm, then into the yo work (p1 tbl, then M1 open-purl), rib to end*.
Slant row 3 (RS) *Rib to 2 sts before slant marker, k2, yo, sm, k1, SKP, rib to end*.
Slant row 4 (WS) *Rib to 3 sts before slant marker, p2tog tbl, p1, sm, then into the yo work (k1 tbl, then M1 open-knit), rib to end*.

Begin Thumb Gusset
Cont to work left slant detail as well as thumb gusset as foll:
Slant row 5 (RS) Rib to 2 sts before slant marker, p2, yo, sm, k1, SKP, rib 21 sts, sm, M1R knitwise, k1, kfb, sm, rib to end.
Row 6 Rib to first thumb gusset marker, sm, p to 2nd thumb gusset marker, sm, rep between *'s of slant row 2.
Row 7 (RS) Rep between *'s of slant row 3, rib to first thumb gusset marker, sm, M1R knitwise, k to 1 st before 2nd thumb gusset marker, kfb, sm, rib to end.
Row 8 (WS) Rib to first thumb gusset marker, sm, p to 2nd thumb gusset marker, sm, rep between *'s of slant row 4.
Row 9 (RS) Work as for slant row 5 only for thumb gusset, sm, M1R knitwise, k to 1 st before 2nd thumb gusset marker, kfb, sm, rib to end.
Rep rows 6–9 until there are 18 sts between thumb gusset markers, end with a WS row.
**At this point, remove slant detail markers and resume working in regular rib as before.
Next row (RS) Work even in rib over 35 sts, M1R, k17, kfb, sm, rib to end.
Next row (WS) Rib 37, p the 20 thumb sts and then place on scrap yarn, rib 35.
Next row (RS) Rib 35, turn work and cast on 6 sts, turn work, rib 37 to end—78 sts.
Cont in k2, p2 rib for 12 rows more.
Change to smaller needles and cont in rib for 6 rows.
Bind off in rib using larger needle.

LEFT MITT
Work as for right mitt, including placement of markers for thumb, up to left slant detail.

Right Slant Detail
Slant row 1 (RS) Rib 62 sts, k2tog, k1, pm, yo, rib to end.
Slant row 2 Rib to the yo, then into the yo work (p1tbl, then M1 open-purl), p1, p2tog, rib to end.
Slant row 3 (RS) Rib to 3 sts before slant marker, k2tog, k1, sm, yo, rib to end.
Slant row 4 Rib to the yo, then into the yo work (k1 tbl, then M1 open-knit), p1, p2tog, rib to end.

Begin Thumb Gusset
Slant row 5 Rib to first thumb gusset marker, sm, M1R knitwise, k1, kfb, sm, rib to 3 sts before slant rib marker, k2tog, k1, sm, yo, rib to end.
Cont to work in this way, foll slant rows 2–5 for slant detail and foll thumb gusset

shaping as for right mitt until there are 18 sts between thumb gusset markers, end with a WS row.
Then, beg at **, complete as for right mitt.

FINISHING
Sew side seams of each mitt.

Thumb
Using dpn, divide 20 thumb sts evenly over 2 dpn, then use a 3rd dpn to pick up and k 8 sts at base of thumb—28 sts. Join and pm for beg of rnd.
Work 4 rnds in k2, p2 rib.
Bind off in rib.
Weave in ends. Steam block lightly.•

Design Note
The diagonal line crossing the ribbing and the stockinette stitch thumb elevate these mitts. Good design is all about the details.

Hourglass Mitts

Easy

MEASUREMENTS
Circumference 6½"/16.5cm
Length 11"/28cm

MATERIALS
Yarn
• 3½oz/100g, 228yd/208m of any DK weight wool in Blue

Needles
• One pair size 6 (4mm) needles, *or size to obtain gauge*

Notions
• Cable needle (cn)
• Stitch markers

GAUGE
21 sts and 34 rows to 4"/10cm over seed st using size 6 (4mm) needles.
TAKE TIME TO CHECK YOUR GAUGE.

STITCH GLOSSARY
3-st RPC Sl 1 st to cn and hold to back, k2, p1 from cn.
3-st LPC Sl 2 sts to cn and hold to front, p1, k2 from cn.
4-st RC Sl 2 sts to cn and hold to back, k2, k2 from cn.

SEED STITCH
(over an odd number of sts)
Row 1 (RS) K1, *p1, k1; rep from * to end.
Row 2 P the knit sts and k the purl sts.
Rep row 2 for seed st.

HOURGLASS CABLE
(over 14 sts)
Row 1 (RS) 3-st LPC, [k1, p1] 4 times, 3-st RPC.
Row 2 K1, p2, [p1, k1] 4 times, p2, k1.
Row 3 P1, 3-st LPC, [p1, k1] 3 times, 3-st RPC, p1.
Row 4 K2, p2, [k1, p1] 3 times, p2, k2.
Row 5 P2, 3-st LPC, [k1, p1] twice, 3-st RPC, p2.
Row 6 K3, p2, [p1, k1] twice, p2, k3.
Row 7 P3, 3-st LPC, p1, k1, 3-st RPC, p3.
Row 8 K4, p2, k1, p3, k4.
Row 9 P4, 3-st LPC, 3-st RPC, p4.
Rows 10, 12, 14, 16, and 18 K5, p4, k5.
Rows 11 and 17 P5, 4-st RC, p5.
Rows 13 and 15 P5, k4, p5.
Row 19 P4, 3-st RPC, 3-st LPC, p4.
Row 20 K4, p2, k1, p3, k4.
Row 21 P3, 3-st RPC, p1, k1, 3-st LPC, p3.
Row 22 K3, p2, [p1, k1] twice, p2, k3.
Row 23 P2, 3-st RPC, [k1, p1] twice, 3-st LPC, p2.
Row 24 K2, p2, [k1, p1] 3 times, p2, k2.
Row 25 P1, 3-st RPC, [p1, k1] 3 times, 3-st LPC, p1.
Row 26 K1, p2, [p1, k1] 4 times, p2, k1.
Row 27 3-st RPC, [k1, p1] 4 times, 3-st LPC.
Row 28 P2, [k1, p1] 5 times, p2.
Rep rows 1–28 for hourglass cable.

NOTE
Hourglass cable may be worked from written instructions or chart.•

LEFT MITT
Cast on 39 sts.
Row 1 K1, *p1, k1; rep from * to end.
Row 2 P1, *k1, p1; rep from * to end.
Rep last 2 rows for k1, p1 rib once more.

Begin Hourglass Cable
Note The 2-st sections on either side of the cable panel are worked in St st, k the knit sts and p the purl sts every row.
Row 1 (RS) K1, p1, k1, pm, k1, p1, pm, work row 1 of cable over 14 sts, pm, p1, k1, pm, work in seed st to last 2 sts, k2tog—38 sts.
Row 2 Work in seed st to marker, sm, p1, k1, sm, work in cable pat as established over 14 sts, sm, k1, p1, sm, work 3 sts in seed st.
Cont in pats as established until 28-row cable pat has been worked 3 times.
Next row (RS) [K1, p1] 10 times, k1, M1 p-st, *k1, p1; rep from * to last st, k1—39 sts.
Cont in k1, p1 rib as established for 3 rows more.
Bind off loosely in rib.

RIGHT MITT
Cast on 39 sts.
Row 1 K1, *p1, k1; rep from * to end.
Row 2 P1, *k1, p1; rep from * to end.
Rep last 2 rows for k1, p1 rib once more.

Begin Hourglass Cable
Note The 2-st sections on either side of the cable panel are worked in St st, k the knit sts and p the purl sts every row.
Row 1 (RS) K2tog, work 16 sts in seed st, pm, k1, p1, pm, work row 1 of cable over 14 sts, pm, p1, k1, pm, work 3 sts in seed st—38 sts.
Row 2 Work 3 sts in seed st, sm, p1, k1, sm, work in cable pat as established over 14 sts, sm, k1, p1, work to end in seed st.
Cont in pats as established until 28-row cable pat has been worked 3 times.
Next row (RS) [K1, p1] 8 times, k1, M1 p-st, *k1, p1; rep from * to last st, k1—39 sts.
Cont in k1, p1 rib as established for 3 rows more.
Bind off loosely in rib.

FINISHING
Sew side seam approx 7¼"/18.5cm from cast-on edge and 2¼"/5.5cm from bound-off edge, leaving approx 1½"/4cm unseamed for thumb opening.
Weave in ends. Block to measurements.•

Design Note
When you find a pattern you love, make sure to show it off! This cable insert runs all the way down the long cuffs, making it stand out even more.

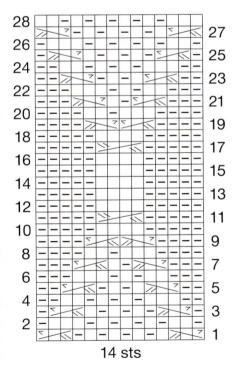

14 sts

STITCH KEY

- ☐ k on RS, p on WS
- − p on RS, k on WS
- 3-st RPC
- 3-st LPC
- 4-st RC

Tiny Bows Wristlets

Easy

MEASUREMENTS
Circumference 4½"/11.5cm
Length 4"/10cm

MATERIALS
Yarn
• 3½oz/100g, 350yd/320m of any fingering weight wool/silk/nylon blend in Pink

Needles
• One set (5) size 2 (2.75mm) double-pointed needles (dpn), *or size to obtain gauge*

Notions
• Stitch markers

GAUGE
32 sts and 36 rnds to 4"/10cm over k3, p1 rib (unstretched) using size 2 (2.75mm) needles.
TAKE TIME TO CHECK YOUR GAUGE.

STITCH GLOSSARY
M1R Insert LH needle from back to front under horizontal strand between the stitch just worked and the next st on LH needle, knit this loop through the front—1 st inc'd.
M1L Insert LH needle from front to back under horizontal strand between the stitch just worked and the next st on LH needle, knit this loop through the back—1 st inc'd.

WRISTLET
Cast on 36 sts and divide sts evenly over 4 dpn. Join, being careful not to twist sts, and pm for beg of rnd.
Rnds 1–6 *K1, p1; rep from * around.
Rnd 7 *K3, p1; rep from * around.
Rep rnd 7 for k3, p1 rib for 3 rnds more.

Shape Thumb
Set-up rnd Work k3, p1 rib over 35 sts, pm, p1, sm—this is end of rnd marker.
Inc rnd 1 Work k3, p1 rib to first marker, sm, M1R, p1, M1L, sm—38 sts.
Rnd 2 Work k3, p1 rib to first marker, sm, k1, p1, k1, sm.
Inc rnd 3 Work k3, p1 rib to first marker, sm, M1R, k1, p1, k1, M1L, sm—40 sts.
Rnd 4 Work k3, p1 rib to first marker, sm, work k1, p1 rib as established to end of rnd, sm.
Inc rnd 5 Work k3, p1 rib to first marker, sm, M1R, work k1, p1 rib to end of rnd, M1L, sm—42 sts.
Rnd 6 Work even in ribs as established.
Inc rnd 7 Work in k3, p1 rib to first marker, sm, M1R, work in k1, p1 to end of rnd, M1L, sm—44 sts.
Rnd 8 Work even in ribs as established.
Rnd 9 Work k3, p1 rib to first marker, remove marker, bind off 9 sts—35 sts.
Next rnd Work in k3, p1 rib over 32 sts, k3, M1 p-st—36 sts.
Cont in k3, p1 rib over all sts as established for 9 rnds more.
Work in k1, p1 rib over all sts for 4 rnds.
Bind off in rib.

FINISHING
Weave in ends. Block lightly.

Bows (make 2)
With 2 dpn, cast on 10 sts. Knit 16 rows. Bind off.
To make bow, wrap a length of yarn tightly around middle of bow.
For right wristlet, sew on bow at ½"/1.5cm from center top with thumb on left.
For left wristlet, sew on bow at ½"/1.5cm from center top with thumb on right.•

Design Note
Short and sweet, these tiny accessories are embellished with adorable bows.

Ribbed Mitts

Intermediate

SIZES
Man's Small/Medium (Large/X-Large). Shown in size Small/Medium.

MEASUREMENTS
Circumference approx 8 (9)"/20.5 (23)cm
Length 8"/20.5cm

MATERIALS
Yarn
• 7oz/198g, 230yd/211m of any worsted weight acrylic in Blue

Needles
• Two circular needles each size 4 and 5 (3.5 and 3.75mm) circular needles, size 32"/80cm long, *or size to obtain gauge*

Notions
• Stitch markers
• Scrap yarn

GAUGE
20 sts and 26 rnds to 4"/10cm over St st using larger needles.
TAKE TIME TO CHECK YOUR GAUGE.

STITCH GLOSSARY
K1-b Knit st in row below.
P1-b Purl st in row below.

NOTES
1) Instructions are given for working in the round on 2 circular needles in order to easily divide the front hand sts (on one needle), which are worked in pat sts, and the palm sts (on the 2nd needle), which are worked in St st.
2) When increasing 1 st at the thumb, work backward loop cast-on method.

FISHERMAN'S RIB PANEL
(over 5 sts)
Rnd 1 [P1, k1-b] twice, p1.
Rnd 2 [P1-b, k1] twice, p1-b.
Rep rnds 1 and 2 for fisherman's rib panel.

CHEVRON PANEL
(over 7 sts)
Rnd 1 K3, p1, k3.
Rnd 2 K2, p1, k1, p1, k2.
Rnd 3 K1, p1, k3, p1, k1.
Rnds 4 and 5 Knit.
Rep rnds 1–5 for chevron panel.

LEFT MITT
With larger needles, cast on 40 (45) sts. Place 17 sts on one needle (for front) and rem 23 (28) sts on 2nd needle (for back). Join to work in rnds, taking care not to twist sts, and pm for beg of rnd.
Rnd 1 *P2, k3; rep from * around.
Rep rnd 1 for p2, k3 rib for 2"/5cm.
Knit 1 rnd.

Begin Patterns
Next rnd Work 17 sts on front needle as foll: work 5 sts in fisherman's rib, work 7 sts in chevron pat, work 5 sts in fisherman's rib; k23 (28) sts on back needle for St st (k every rnd).
Cont in pats as established until piece measures 4"/10cm from beg.

Begin Thumb Gusset
Next rnd Cont pat over 17 sts of front needle; on back needle k to last 3 (5) sts, pm, cast on 1 st, k1, cast on 1 st, pm, k2 (4).
Next rnd Work in pat to next marker, sm, cast on 1 st, k to next marker, cast on 1 st, sm, k2 (4).
Rep last rnd 5 (6) times more—there are 15 (17) sts between thumb markers.
Next rnd Cont pat over 17 sts of front needle; on back needle k to marker, remove marker, place 15 (17) thumb sts on scrap yarn, remove marker, cast on 1 st, k2 (4)—40 (45) sts.
Work even in pats until piece measures 7"/17.5cm from beg, or 1"/2.5cm less than desired length. Knit 1 rnd over all sts.
Change to smaller needles.
Work in p2, k3 rib as before for 1"/2.5cm.
Bind off in rib.

Thumb
Place 15 (17) sts from holder on needles, pick up and k 5 sts at base of thumb to close gap—20 (22) sts. Divide sts over two needles—10 (11) sts on each needle.
Join and work in St st for 1 (1¼)"/2.5 (3)cm, or desired length.
Bind off loosely.

RIGHT MITT
Work as for left mitt to thumb gusset.

Begin Thumb Gusset
Next rnd Cont pat over 17 sts of front needle; on back needle, k2 (4), pm, cast on 1 st, k1, cast on 1 st, pm, k to end.
Next rnd Work in pat to marker, sm, cast on 1 st, k to next marker, cast on 1 st, sm, k to end.
Rep last rnd 5 (6) times more—there are 15 (17) sts between thumb markers.
Next rnd Cont in pat over 17 sts of front needle; on back needle k2 (4), remove marker, place 15 (17) sts on scrap yarn, remove marker, cast on 1 st, k to end—40 (45) sts.
Complete same as left mitt.•

Design Note
While this pattern calls for working over two circular needles (which many knitters enjoy), you can divide the sts over 3 or 4 dpn and work that way, disregarding notes about front and back needles.

Fur-Trimmed Mitts

Intermediate

SIZES
Small/Medium (Large/X-Large).
Shown in Small/Medium.

MEASUREMENTS
Circumference 6¾ (7¾)"/17 (19.5)cm
Length 6¾"/17cm

MATERIALS
Yarn
- 5oz/142g, 251yd/230m of any worsted weight acrylic in Blue (A) (4)
- 1¾oz/50g, 64yd/58m of any chunky weight eyelash in Blue (B) (5)

Needles
- One set (4) size 8 (5mm) double-pointed needles (dpn), *or size to obtain gauge*

Notions
- Cable needle (cn)
- Stitch marker
- Scrap yarn

GAUGE
20 sts and 28 rnds to 4"/10cm over cable/eyelet pat using size 8 (5mm) needles.
TAKE TIME TO CHECK YOUR GAUGE.

STITCH GLOSSARY
6-st BC Sl 3 sts to cn and hold to back, k3, k3 from cn
6-st FC Sl 3 sts to cn and hold to front, k3, k3 from cn

CABLE/EYELET PATTERN FOR LEFT MITT
(multiple of 11 sts plus 5)
Rnds 1, 3, 5, and 7 Knit.
Rnd 2 *Yo, ssk, k1, k2tog, yo, k6; rep from * once more, yo, ssk, k1, k2tog, yo.
Rnd 4 K1, *yo, SK2P, yo, k1, 6-st BC, k1; rep from * once more, yo, SK2P, yo, k1.
Rnd 6 Rep rnd 2.
Rnd 8 K1, *yo, SK2P, yo, k8; rep from * once more, yo, SK2P, yo, k1.
Rep rnds 1–8 for cable/eyelet pat for left mitt.

CABLE/EYELET PATTERN FOR RIGHT MITT
(multiple of 11 sts plus 5)
Rnds 1, 3, 5, and 7 Knit.
Rnd 2 *Yo, ssk, k1, k2tog, yo, k6; rep from * once more, yo, ssk, k1, k2tog, yo.
Rnd 4 K1, *yo, SK2P, yo, k1, 6-st FC, k1; rep from * once more, yo, SK2P, yo, k1.
Rnd 6 Rep rnd 2.
Rnd 8 K1, *yo, SK2P, yo, k8; rep from * once more, yo, SK2P, yo, k1.
Rep rnds 1–8 for cable/eyelet pat for right mitt.

LEFT MITT
With B, cast on 33 (39) sts. Divide sts evenly over 3 needles—11 (13) sts on each needle. Join, taking care not to twist sts, and pm for beg of rnd.
Knit 12 rnds. Change to A and knit 2 rnds.

Beg Cable/Eyelet Pattern
Rnd 1 K1 (3), work cable/eyelet pat for left mitt over next 27 sts, k5 (9).
Cont in pat as established, working sts outside of the cable/eyelet pat in St st (k every rnd) until 8 rnds of pat have been worked 3 times (24 rnds in pat).

Thumb Gusset
Next rnd Work in pat to last 5 (7) sts, k1 (3), M1, k3, M1, k1—35 (41) sts.
Note Work inc sts in St st.
Work 1 rnd even.
Next rnd Work in pat to last 7 (9) sts, k1 (3), M1, k5, M1, k1—37 (43) sts.
Work 1 rnd even.
Next rnd Work in pat to last 9 (11) sts, k1 (3), M1, k7, M1, k1—39 (45) sts.
Work 1 rnd even.
Next rnd Work in pat to last 11 (13) sts, k1 (3), M1, k9, M1, k1—41 (47) sts.
Work 1 rnd even.
Next rnd Work in pat to last 13 (15) sts, k1 (3), M1, k11, M1, k1—43 (49) sts.
Work 1 rnd even.

For size Large/X-Large only
Next rnd Work in pat to last 15 sts, k3, M1, k11, M1, k1—51 sts.
Work 1 rnd even.

For both sizes
Next rnd Work in pat to last 14 (16) sts, slip next 13 (15) sts to scrap yarn for thumb, cast on 1 st, k1—31 (37) sts.
Cont in pat as established, working 4 (10) sts outside of cable/eyelet pat in St st, until 8 rnds of pat have been worked a total of 6 times from beg. Bind off loosely.

Thumb
Slip 13 (15) sts from scrap yarn to needle, pick up and k 1 st at base of the thumb to

close the gap—14 (16) sts. Divide sts evenly over 3 needles.
Join and knit 4 rnds.
Bind off loosely.

RIGHT MITT
With B, cast on 33 (39) sts. Divide sts evenly over 3 needles—11 (13) sts on each needle. Join to work in rnds, and pm for beg of rnd.
Knit 12 rnds. Change to A and knit 2 rnds.

Beg Cable/Eyelet Pattern
Rnd 1 K5 (9), work cable/eyelet pat for right mitt over next 27 sts, k1 (3). Cont in pat as established, working sts outside of the cable/eyelet pat in St st (k every rnd) until 8 rnds of pat have been worked 3 times (24 rnds in pat).

Thumb gusset
Next rnd K1, M1, k3, M1, k1 (5), work in pats as established over 27 sts, k1 (3)—35 (41) sts.
Complete to correspond to left mitt, reversing thumb incs as established.•

Design Note
Sometimes more is more! Combine lace, cables, and a fun faux-fur trim for a pair of playful mitts that are sure to make you smile.

Eyelet Rib Wristers

●● Easy

SIZE
Will stretch to fit most.

MEASUREMENTS
Circumference (unstretched)
5"/12.5cm
Length 6"/15.5cm

MATERIALS
Yarn
• 1¾oz/50g, 117yd/107m of any DK weight superwash wool/acrylic/nylon blend in Green

Needles
• One pair size 6 (4mm) needles, *or size to obtain gauge*

GAUGE
26 sts and 28 rows to 4"/10cm over eyelet rib using size 6 (4mm) needles.
TAKE TIME TO CHECK YOUR GAUGE.

EYELET RIB
(multiple of 6 sts plus 3)
Row 1 (RS) K1 (selvage st), k1, *yo, k1, k3tog, k1, yo, k1; rep from * to last st, k1 (selvage st).
Row 2 P1 (selvage st), p1, *k5, p1; rep from * to last st, p1 (selvage st).
Rep rows 1 and 2 for eyelet rib.

WRISTLET
Cast on 33 sts.
Row 1 (RS) P1, *k1, p1; rep from * to end.
Cont in k1, p1 rib as established for 3 rows more.
Work in eyelet rib until piece measures 5½"/14cm from beg, end with a WS row.
Next row (RS) P1, *k1, p1; rep from * to end.
Cont in k1, p1 rib as established for 3 rows more.
Bind off in rib.

FINISHING
Fold wristlet in half lengthwise. Beg at lower edge, sew side seam for 3½"/9cm, leave next 1"/2.5cm unsewn for thumb opening, sew rem 1½"/4cm to close wristlet.
Weave in ends. Block lightly. •

Design Note
The lace pattern in these wristlets have extra stretch, making them perfect when fitting a range of sizes.

Techniques

3-Needle Bind-Off

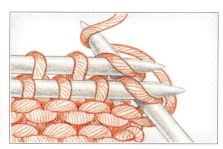

1) Hold right sides of pieces together on two needles. Insert third needle knitwise into first st of each needle, and wrap yarn knitwise.

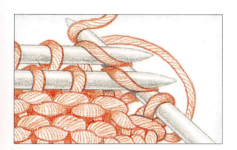

2) Knit these two sts together, and slip them off the needles. *Knit the next two sts together in the same manner.

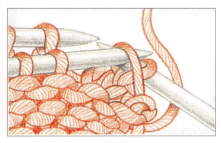

3) Slip first st on 3rd needle over 2nd st and off needle. Rep from * in step 2 across row until all sts are bound off.

Kitchener Stitch

Cut a tail at least 4 times the length of the edge that will be grafted together and thread through a tapestry needle. Hold needles together with right sides showing, making sure each has the same number of live stitches, and work as follows:

 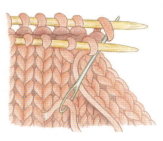

1) Insert tapestry needle purlwise through first stitch on front needle. Pull yarn through, leaving stitch on needle.

2) Insert tapestry needle knitwise through first stitch on back needle. Pull yarn through, leaving stitch on needle.

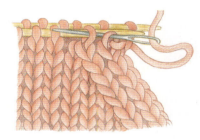 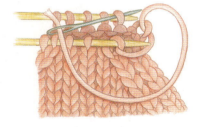

3) Insert tapestry needle knitwise through first stitch on front needle, pull yarn through, and slip stitch off needle. Then, insert tapestry needle purlwise through next stitch on front needle and pull yarn through, leaving this stitch on needle.

4) Insert tapestry needle purlwise through first stitch on back needle, pull yarn through, and slip stitch off needle. Then, insert tapestry needle knitwise through next stitch on back needle and pull yarn through, leaving this stitch on needle.

Repeat steps 3 and 4 until all stitches on both front and back needles have been grafted.

Embroidery Stitches

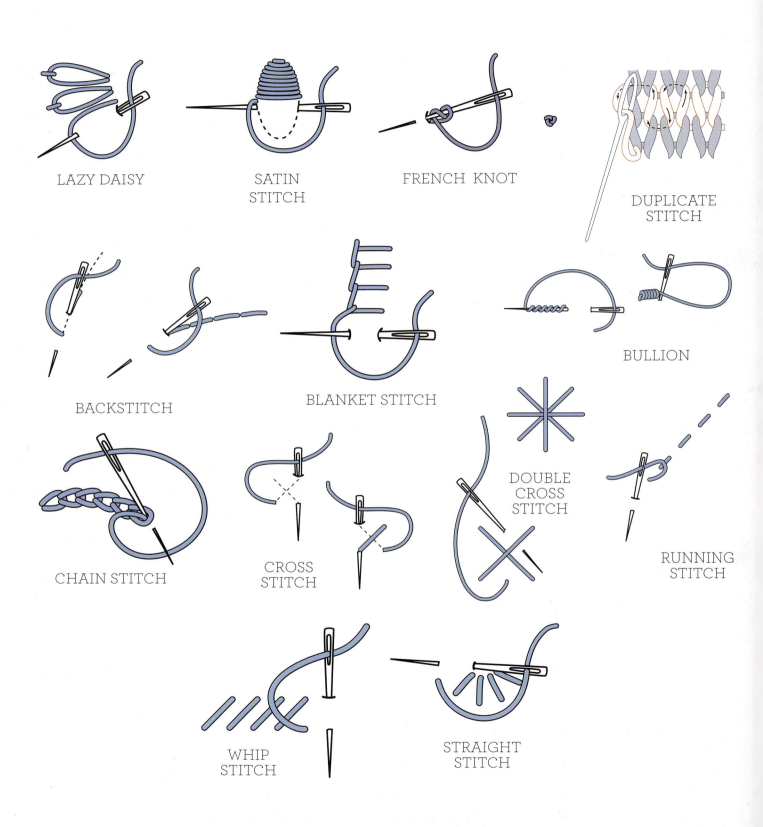